Letters From Prison

D.E. Whitchurch III

To Sidney
Best Wishes in All You Do

Copyright © 2007 by D.E. Whitchurch III

All rights reserved. No part of this book shall be reproduced or transmitted in any form or by any means, electronic, mechanical, magnetic, photographic including photocopying, recording or by any information storage and retrieval system, without prior written permission of the publisher. No patent liability is assumed with respect to the use of the information contained herein. Although every precaution has been taken in the preparation of this book, the publisher and author assume no responsibility for errors or omissions. Neither is any liability assumed for damages resulting from the use of the information contained herein.

ISBN 0-7414-3904-2

Published by:

1094 New DeHaven Street, Suite 100
West Conshohocken, PA 19428-2713
Info@buybooksontheweb.com
www.buybooksontheweb.com
Toll-free (877) BUY BOOK
Local Phone (610) 941-9999
Fax (610) 941-9959

Printed in the United States of America

Printed on Recycled Paper

Published April 2007

Introduction

In the summer of 1995, I lived along highway 101 in the small northern California town of Redcrest, just thirty five miles south of Eureka. A young woman, whom I will call Michelle, found herself with car problems on the highway off ramp next to my home. When I noticed her predicament, two of Humboldt County's most squalid bikers were volunteering their full, but capricious attention.

Having known this road scum for twenty years, I was sure any assistance came with a price.

Due to my early years as a hell raiser, (I did my time as the prodigal son, astride two wheels) our would be heros and I had locked horns more than once. My two former confederates were unsure if a wife and family had made me soft. To my surprise and relief, they were reluctant to find out for sure. Not to go into much detail, or self incrimination, our good Samaritans came to a salubrious decision to leave the young woman in my capable hands. I suspect the pair of Rottweiler's, in the back of my truck, might have helped tilt the scales in my favor.

I waited with Michelle, while her car was being repaired, and she expressed her intention to attend Humboldt State in the fall. She'd been to see the campus earlier that day and was on her way home to the San Francisco Bay area, when her car broke down.

Over the next few months, Michelle stopped by our house frequently, having become close friends with my oldest daughter. Then, as suddenly as she came into our lives, her visits ended.

It wasn't until my daughter received a letter from Michelle that we realized why she hadn't been by. In the corner was a red stamp: State Prison.

As fate would have it, while attending Humboldt State, Michelle found herself in the wrong crowd, transporting the area's most prolific crop, Marijuana.

I think the most distressing thing to me was that Michelle was from a wealthy family and, other than the raw excitement of committing a crime, I couldn't understand why she would put herself in this position. But this wasn't as perturbing to me as the fact that her parents had deserted her. Her father moved to New York, and her mother flew off to Europe, both running away, to avoid the embarrassment of their daughter's incarceration.

During the time Michelle had spent in our home, I found myself taken by her innocence and charm, to the point of becoming a surrogate father.

Up till that point in my life, I had never been much on writing letters, but the joy Michelle expressed at each of my letters kept me pecking at the keyboard of my laptop.

It wasn't long before I found myself getting letters from other women in Michelle's facility. They all liked the pictures I sent and the stories of my day to day life. When you're a truck driver, traveling to every state in the lower forty eight, your travels and pictures become greedily anticipated by those whose worlds have been reduced to twenty acres of razor wire and concrete.

After Michelle's release from prison, I continued writing to a couple of inmates but, after their subsequent release, I put down my lap top and thought nothing more about it.

A few years later, my wife and I began kicking around the idea of getting off the road and opening a sports bar and restaurant. Even though I love driving a big rig, twenty five years and two and a half million miles were taking their toll. We'd examined the possibilities and potential of various areas around the country and had done a fair amount of research. Time and time again, we came

Letters from Prison

back to the major factor in the success of such a venture – the employees who would interact directly with the customers.

In July of 1999, we stopped at a travel plaza on the Pennsylvania turnpike. Needing coffee, I walked up to the counter at a Starbucks and was greeted by one of the most unpleasant young women I've ever met. When I asked what was bothering her, I was told, "I just don't want to be here."

I frowned a bit. "Did you come here and fill out an application?" I asked.

"Yeah. How else do you think I got the job?" Her voice was full of disgust.

"Do you realize that the person who employed you has entrusted you with the success or failure of his livelihood?" She ignored me. "I'll bet your daddy made you come down here, get a job, and maybe learn some responsibility," I said.

She shoved my coffee unceremoniously toward my side of the counter and slammed the cash register drawer shut. "Have a nice day," she said with venom in her voice.

Back in the truck, relating the incident to my wife, my mind drifted back to the letters I'd received from the young women in prison, some not much older than the disagreeable young woman at the counter. Thinking of the joy they expressed over a simple letter, from a person they didn't even know, spawned an idea.

I pondered the issue of employees for the sports bar once again. In this day of political correctness, I wanted the women who worked for me to be pleasant and attractive, yet have slightly thick skin. I wanted them to be able to handle the clientele with finesse and humor, not scream, "Sexual Harassment," every time some clown patted them on the bottom. I wanted employees who were sassy, but not rude. Most of all I wanted employees who enjoyed their jobs and wanted to be at work.

I considered the women in prison, with whom I'd shared several months of correspondence. Time and again, they'd made it clear they wanted a second chance and hoped they'd be able to find employment when they got out.

I did a little research and proposed my plan to my wife, explaining how I wanted to locate female inmates, who might be potential employees for our future restaurant enterprise.

"Are you out of your mind?" My wife is obviously very direct and concise.

"No, listen. I can go on the internet and locate woman who are in prison. The web sites I've checked usually list the inmates age, crime and previous occupation, as well as posting a picture. If we can find women who are currently serving short sentences for minor crimes and who've been in the hospitality industry, we might find some great future employees. We're three or four years from getting off the road, so we've got plenty of time to contact maybe fifteen or twenty women, get to know them through correspondence and even visit them in prison, if we think they're possible candidates. That gives them time to get to know and respect us and gives them some hope for a future when they're released."

After some further discussion and debate, it was agreed that I would locate and contact a dozen or more possible prospects. I'd heard about the JailBabes website and it seemed to be the primary site for contacting prison pen pales. After a great deal of time and research, I prepared an introductory letter and sent it out to twenty women, hoping three or four might prove to be potentially good employees and interested in our adventure. I included two women who were not candidates, as they were serving life terms. One reason was, admittedly, curiosity and the second reasons was my growing suspicion that many of the female inmates might not have been behind bars, without the negative influence of a man or men in their lives.

My first letter to each inmate was basically the same, with some minor modifications.

Letters from Prison

Dear _____

I saw your profile on the Jail Babes website, where you said you were interested in finding pen pals. I want you to know I'm not looking for a soul mate, just someone to be a pen pal with. For reasons of my own, I am contacting several women who are currently incarcerated. I was drawn to your ad for two reasons. Your profile is interesting and your photo is attractive.

I'm a long haul trucker, who enjoys sailing, golf, martial arts and almost anything that involves the outdoors. Enclosed is a picture of me, along with some places I've been. If you find me the least bit interesting or you're just plain bored, drop me a note. I would be happy to be your pen pal.

Sincerely,

In my second letter, I related Michelle's story, explaining that knowing how much letters and news from the outside had meant to her, I'd decided to contact others in prison facilities. I sometimes mentioned my experience with the girl at the Starbucks counter. It wasn't until I had a better idea of my correspondents that I broached the issue of the proposed sports bar and grill.

Letters from Prison is a compilation of the responses I received from the women I contacted, who were in correctional facilities in various parts of the country. Some of the letters were from cell mates or friends of my initial contacts.

The letters are included as they were originally written, without benefit of editorial corrections to grammar, spelling or sentence structure. Each woman has a separate chapter of the book and the order in which they appear is based on the order in which they first responded to my introductory letter.

Unfortunately, fate intervened in our plans for the sports bar and we were forced to postpone pursuing our dream, a fact I shared with the women, as soon as I realized the situation.

Gradually, most of the women dropped the correspondence, as you will see. I leave it to you to ascertain their initial and continuing sincerity, their interest in potential employment and their pursuit of their own needs and desires. Were they looking for a pen pal, a source of financial assistance or an old man into whom they might get their hooks, for future gain and benefit? You decide.

Alison

NDOC Women's Prison, Las Vegas, Nevada

March 6, 2001
Dear Ed,

It was nice to receive your letter in the mail. It's a shock to see that your from Eugene. That's where I'm from. I lived in Eugene for 14 years. I just moved from there a little over a year ago. All my family still lives there and that is where I'll be moving back to when I'm released   So hopefully we do become good friends - maybe more. Than we can get together and have some fun. So, you're a sailor, huh? That's one thing I've never done, but definitely want to try. The closest I've ever come was jet skiing at Orchard Point!! I also like to golf, although I'm not very good at it. Maybe you could give me a few pointers.

I would love to see you next time you come to town. I never get visitors. I could really use a good friend.

A little about me, I am outgoing, open, honest and loving. I like to cook, swim, do anything outdoors and just have fun. I'm studying to get my degree in Paralegal right now. Should be done by next year

Well I hope you write back, I'd love to hear from you again!

Take care, and sleep with the angels!

Sincerely, Alison

PS. We can't receive stamps here, but thank you anyway!

Letters from Prison

Author's Note:

Alison's bio stated she had been an exotic dancer. She was also an attractive woman. I felt she might be a possible addition to my nightclub venture. If a woman could deal with a number of groping men with her clothes off, then a few obnoxious men during Monday Night Football shouldn't be a problem. Of course, if she finished her paralegal studies, my future offer probably wouldn't be needed.

I had done some background work on several of the women, prior to writing, and already knew Alison was from Eugene. I felt this to be a plus, as Eugene was where I intended to open the sports bar.

March 13, 2001

Hello again! How are you today? I am doing okay, I just have been a little stressed lately - I guess summer is coming soon and I'm trying to do a lot so I can relax by then.

I will enclose a visiting form for you to fill out and just mail it back with your next letter and as soon as it is approved I will let you know, so you can make arrangements to come down. It would be really nice to see you.

In my picture that you saw, I am wearing a tank top -- that's all. I updated my pictures on Jail Babes.com in case you want to take a look. I think you'd be impressed!!

To answer you question about Vegas. I've never lived here. I moved to Reno last December (1999) and I used to be a dancer (something I'm not very proud of) that's when I got into trouble. The only reason I'm in Vegas is because this is where the prison is.

When I get out, I'd like to check-out Vegas, but I don't think I'd ever live here. This place is way to much for me. I like Eugene! That's where I want to live my life out! I want to retire being a Duck

I would love to go sailing with you. What kind of boat do you have? Where do you sail at? Do you have any kids? The Harley would be fun too! If it's not raining!

Well I'd better go so I can mail this out.

Take care and write back soon!

Love, Alison

April 15, 2001

Happy Easter!

Dear Ed,

Hello there! How is your day going so far? I hope it is good. My Easter has been okay, considering my predicament!! I spent most of the day working on my tan. It been about 87° all day. So I had to take advantage of the sun.

I did recognize the trucking co. in your picture. I've seen lots of those trucks around Eugene. I've probably seen you and we just didn't know each other then!

I hope the unloading in Santa Cruz went okay! It didn't sound like very much fun.

I wish you could of stopped in when you were here. Fill out the visiting form I enclosed and as soon as it comes back I'll let you know. I'm always good for a laugh. And I'm sure we would have a good time. And don't worry, I wont' tease you. I know how hard that can be, and there is nothing I can do about it while I'm in here.

Thanks for the understanding of my "former life". Your right it does take a lot of nerve to get up there. But after a while you just kind of tune everything out and try to make it thru your shift. Bachelor parties are much easier because the crowd is usually very easy to please. I bet the girl at the Silver Dollar really felt special when you commented on her smile. That always makes you remember that there are still some good men left - and you must be one of them.

> *How far do you travel on your job? Do you come to Vegas much? What are your plans for summer?*
>
> *Well I'd better run for now, it's dinner time. Take care of yourself - I hope to hear from you soon. And don't worry there aren't any toys in here. At least none that I know of - But who knows !*
>
> *Love, Alison*

Author's Note:

So far, Alison seemed to be a likely candidate for the sports bar.

April 18, 2001
Dear Ed,

Hello again! How's your day today? Mine has been fair. Kind of stressful though. I just found out that NDOP is garnishing my inmate account for court fines & fees. They took all of my money off of my account. So now I don't have anything left. I know it's a lot to ask, but if it is possible, do you think you could help me out. Any amount would be very helpful. I enclosed a deposit coupon all you have to do is send it to the circled address w/ a money order. I thought I could pay these fines when I was released, but I guess I learned the hard way. The prison already takes 10% of all our money and now they are going to take 50% of all my deposits for fines. So that only leaves me 40% to buy necessities.

Other than that, things are going well. I have a class tonight at 6pm w/ John Ross. Have you heard of him? He is a motivational speaker. He's great. Well I'd better get ready for class.

Love, Alison
PS. When is your Birthday?

Letters from Prison

Author's Note:

In the research I did, prior to contacting the inmates listed on JailBabes, one of the consistent warnings was the women were often looking for pen pals who would supplement whatever money they might have. While I knew that many of those incarcerated were short of funds, unless they had a wealthy family to provide assistance, I'd hoped to be something more than a lending institution. Here was the first indication that Alison, at least, had her own agenda and priorities.

May 5, 2001
Dear Ed,

Hello there. Happy Cinco De Mayo!

You letter was a nice surprise. I feel like I'm getting to know more about you. That was a great reason that you have for writing inmates. I can fully relate. When I get your letters it brightens my day. Especially since your from Eugene. It's like hearing from a friend back home. I do consider you a true friend. You are such a sweet, noble person to give your time and feelings to someone whom you've never met. I appreciate it. It gets very lonely in here and you make my days brighter when I hear from you.

I will be interested to know your other reasons too. But I will wait patiently for you to be ready to tell me the third reason.

Thank you very much for sending me the money. I can't thank you enough. It will be very helpful. I got your visiting form and turned it into my councelor. He said they take a few weeks to come back. So I'll let you know as soon as I hear something. I can't wait until you can stop in to see me. I bet you will make me smile. You seem very easy to get along with. The company will be nice. How often do you come to Vegas?

> *So, how are things in Eugene? Has there been much rain. I bet the air smells nice. That's one thing I miss so much, just the smell of the trees and flowers. Here it just smells like smog and dust. There aren't any pretty mountains covered with trees to look at. I can't wait to come home.*
>
> *Well, it's getting late. I'll be waiting for your next letter. Have a safe and happy week.*
>
> Your friend, Alison

Author's Note:

You're right. I'm an easy touch. I sent the woman twenty five dollars, hoping she was genuine, and someone I could employ.

May 28, 2001

Dear Ed,

> *Hi there! How are you? I'm doing good. Sorry it has taken me so long to write you back. I know that you don't normally write people who have as little time as me, but I am very glad that you did because I think of you as a great friend. The fact that we are both from Eugene is so weird. Maybe we were meant to cross paths*
>
> *I think your ideas that you have for the sports bar are great! I know what you mean by the over-sensitive girl! As you already know, I used to be a dancer and even when girls worked there, they used to complain about guys hitting on them!! Hello! That's what they are there for. I think the idea is great and if it takes shape, I'd love to work there. I could definatly recommend some people for you. No sissies!*

Letters from Prison

> *So how has work been going lately? Are you covering a lot of ground? I hope your not dying in the heat. It's been miserable here. I wish it would rain for just one day! I really miss the weather in Oregon. But not too long and I'll be back. Probably getting mad because it's raining too much!!*
>
> *I'm enclosing the deposit coupon for next time. Thanks again for all your help and support Ed. More people need to have someone like you on their side.*
>
> *Write back soon!*
>
> *Love, Alison*

Author's Note:

As you can see, I shared with her my intentions of opening a sports bar and restaurant. I also told her she would be a candidate to work there. She seemed excited, but almost in the same breath asked, "Hey, you got any money to send me?" The enclosed deposit coupon was less than subtle. My skepticism about Alison began to grow.

June 7, 2001
Dear Ed,

Hi, it's me again. I just wanted to write you a quick letter, just to say hi and to let you know that your visiting application was approved.

My councelor told me yesterday. When do you think that you'll be in Las Vegas again? I hope you will be able to stop in and visit me, even for a little while.

I can't wait, I know we will get along great.

Well, I'd better go. Write back when you can. Take care of yourself.

Love from, Alison

Letters from Prison

Author's Note:

Well, it appeared I might meet a possible future "Pirate's Cove" employee and maybe get a better reading on whether she was interested in her future or my current monetary support.

July 10, 2001
Dear Ed,

It was nice to get your letter today. I'm glad to hear you had a nice trip. I'm really sorry that you had such horrible news waiting for you when you got back.

I really hope you get things straightened out so you can get your plans for your club on their way. I think your club will be a big success!

I can't wait to meet you. I hope you'll be able to drop in soon. It's okay for you to wear Black wranglers, just not blue ones.

Not much is going on around here. The same stuff, just a different day! The weather here is miserable. I miss the warm summers in Eugene. Here it is hotter than hot. I hate it. I can't wait to be back in Eugene. I just want to see some rain!

I hope you had a nice 4th of July. We had a BBQ - the food was actually good! But no fireworks!! Oh well! Write back soon. Be safe & I hope to see you soon.

Love, Alison

Author's Note:

As you can see, I shared with Alison the news about the sports bar being postponed, until I could straighten out my difficulties with the IRS. In my response to this letter, I explained I could no longer send her money and that the sports bar was on hold indefinitely. I never got another letter and I never went to meet her.

Jennifer W.

Dept. of Criminal Justice, Institutional Division

Marlin, TX

March 24, 2001
Daniel or Ed,
Hello there. I received your most welcomed missive last week! Sorry it takes me a while to return your letter. I've been having one of my moments. Ha' Ha'. Im glad you find me attractive and interesting, thank you! I find you very attractive, that salt & pepper beard, I love it! I just want to cuddle up with you, a big teddy bear! I can tell you what, right now being locked up is the least of my recent problems.
In Dec. my house burnt down, lost everything, then in Feb my mother-totaled my mothers car and almost died! Things are looking up now! My mother is doing great my mom got a new car, she don't have a new house, but she's decided o live w/my grandma for a while! Its been a wild ride, the bad thing about my house was my 5 yr old son did it. My mom didn't have insurance on anything! Thank God Im a very stable person, a survivor! I must admit Im jealous of you on that boat, I want to be there. I love the water. Im scared of what is in the water, but I love it! I love the beach. I'll spend my whole summer in a g-string on the beach! I cant play golf, as a matter of fact Im like "Happy Gilmore" when it comes to golf! Ha! Now Harleys, I love bikes. I was raised on the back of a bike, my sisters dad is the president of the Gypsys! Im not a biker chick though!

> I've always wanted to travel around the U S in an 18 wheeler, but I've never had the chance. I have two wonderful kids, a 5 yr old son Zane and a 2yr old girl Sydnie, my babies! I don't get to see them, but I do write them always, It kills me not to see them but God will fix it! I have 8 tattoo, had 18 piercings! Im a freak! I like flea markets, antiques, car shows, fishing, camping, hunting, sitting at home! Im not a picky person, I'm very open minded and easy going as well. Im done for now, hope to hear from you!
>
> As Always, Jennifer.
>
> PS. Is it PO Box 21537 or 31537?

Author's Note:

    Had I known she had 18 piercings, Jennifer would not have been a candidate. Nonetheless, I would continue to answer any letters she sent.

> April 18, 2001
> Ed,
>
>   Hello! Sorry I've taken so long! I got a new job and Im working 4-10s's and its kicking my little ass. Ha! How have you been? Did you have a good Easter? Well, Im okay!
>
>   My sister and man came to see me on Sat. we had a good visit, but the 3 of us have no business being together at the same time! Ha! That was the first time in years that we've been in the same room together! It was nice though. Im so not talkative, Im so tired, but I feel bad for not writing! I like to write people back! But I'm dog tired, so this is extremely short! I hop you done mind!
>
> As Always, Jennifer

Letters from Prison

May 26, 2001
Howdy Ed,

Sorry Im taken forever! Man Im stuck in a stupior (sp). I can't seem to come out of the blues! My man is seriously pissing me off. So how are you doing? My mom did however make my Mothers Day wonderful. She went to Austin and picked up my son & brother and brought them to see me! I havent seen my son since Dec. and my brother since July of last year. Me & my brother are so close, so close in fact that he has a baby due in Nov. and if it's a girl hes naming her Jennifer Lynn after me! Yeah! I love my brother so much, my son he is just the shit! Well its ben several days since I wrote! Well another weekend has passed and no one has come to see me or has not written me to tell me about my daughter, so I have no idea if Ill get to ever see my little girl again! If my husband lost custody, then I wont see her until she is 18, or when I get out! Im very, very pissed off right now! My mother knows how important it is for me to know about my daughter, yet she doesn't write me or come see me! I can't handle this. Im going to have a nervous breakdown over my kids! No one seems to understand how important they really are to me! So Im still mad at my mom to top it all off, she doesn't ever remember to send me money. I don't like to be poor. Its to hard in here to be broke! It depresses me even more! I need a coke! So how was your Memorial weekend? I sure miss going to the lake or the beach and getting totally lit up! If Im at the beach, it's a cooler full of beer! I like Coors Lite, but I started drinking Bud Light before I got locked up! Id rather have Zuma or Crown, Yum-yum Crown!!! Make my mouth water. Well Ed, Im gonna end this for now! Hope to hear from you soon!

As Always,
Jennifer

Letters from Prison

> *Hey will you look up www.funnyshit.com And send me some of the priceless jokes! I think they are way to funny! Pretty, pretty please!*

Author's Note:

Okay, here's the hint about money. I'd hoped she might be looking for a pen pal, not a banker. She's the second contact who responded to my introductory letter and the second request for funds. I began to understand the warnings I read and heard.

June 30, 2001
Ed,

Howdy! How are you? Me Im pretty groovy. Once again sorry for taking so long. You know how women are, full of excuses? Or wait maybe thats men! Ha! I've been working on my appeals so I've gotten behind on everything! Now I love your motor scooter, Im really wanting to go for a ride, so can I? I love the colors! I think the idea you have for the Bar & Grill is wonderfull. I've worked for a Bar & Grill and a Sports bar and I loved my job. I loved all the men and their attention more! Of course Im a little cute thing w/blonde hair and some short kacki shorts, but I hear you on the sexual harassment, but personally I think it's a crock of shit, its just another reason for women to make themselves look weak! I think the only way Id ever persue (sp) sex - harassment is if I were raped, other than that I ask for my attention, plus Im woman enough to tell him Id kick his ass, if he pushes me and still look cute as hell doing it! Ha! I think it is a wonderful idea. Id be kinda wary though to be honest. I've met some seriously crooked chicks in here. But hey Id be perfect for the place! I'd come work for you! Of course I have to be the owners pet! Im so bad!

> *Ha!!! Now about that web-site, yes we can have pornography, we get Penthouse and shit here, so I don't see the difference. My friend sent me a few of them off the site with no trouble! So whats up for July 4th!? I hope you don't have to work! Have a cold beer for me! Well Im gonna head out. You be careful out there!*
>
> As Always
Jennifer

Author's Note:

Ah, Jennifer is now warning me of the treacherous women who can be found in the prison system. You'll notice, however, she's careful to point out she's not one of them.

This was the last letter I received from Jennifer W. I never sent her money, but she never directly asked for any. I also never sent her the porn she wanted off the internet. Perhaps she found someone more cooperative.

Connie

State Prison, Chowchilla, CA

March 26, 2001
Dear Ed,

Well hello there, thank you so much for writing. Matter of fact you're the first person who has responded to my ad. Believe me my self esteem has been bruised

Yes its' true I sure am having a difficult time in here to say the least, I hate it.

It sounds like you write a lot of girls? As for me you'll be my only pen pal. So you like Harleys !! So do I. You sound really out going & interesting. Tell me more. So you live in Eugene huh? I used to live in Brookings, Oregon. And wish I'd never left. Oregon is beautiful, my mother is my only living relative and she still loves in Oregon. Your photo of the ocean really made me homesick !!

I want you to know Ed, whatever questions you ask I'll always answer, I have nothing to hide. I'm very straight up, open minded and believe just because I made a left instead of a right   I'm still human and deserve to be cared for. I'm a loyal true friend and promise to be a fun pen pal! I'd love a visit Ed, let me know and I'll send you the visiting form. I have more likes than dislikes, and seriously need someone in my life right now who understands. Waiting to hear from you. I <u>promise</u> our next letters will be more interesting. I'm nervous !! with this first one (smile).

Letters from Prison

> *Have a great day Ed.*
> *Always, Connie*

Author's Note:

Connie seemed real to me, open and honest about her incarceration, and I sensed a hint of loneliness. Besides, I have a soft spot for Brookings, Oregon, where I went to elementary school and bought hamburgers at the A & W for ten cents. I sent Connie some stationary and things she might need to keep writing.

> *May 2, 2001*
> *Dear Ed,*
>
> *Hello my friend ! I can't thank you enough for the beautiful stationary, I love it. Really thank you so much. It's amazing how such little things have so much meaning.*
>
> *So how did your trip to Tempe go? I really like it there, I used to visit friends in Mesa I stayed there once for about 3 months. My other friend even owned a small landscape business in Apache Junction. Now that was really in the middle of no where   I think your sailing trips sound so cool. Now thats the life Ed.*
>
> *It's funny you should comment on your opinion about 80% of the women locked up. Because honest to God, thats <u>really</u> what happened to me! It hasn't been easy learning to survive up in here when you have no one out there. I think back to when my whole world fell apart, and yes Ed it was because of a very abusive relationship. The stories I could tell you, and I'm sure I will one of these days...When the time is right.*

Letters from Prison

When you mentioned Hanscombs Market!! Now there's no need to ask my Aunt. I myself remember Hanscombs, I loved that store, I even had a charge there. You know back in the days where everybody knew everybody else and had trust. They carried all of the Levis and real good work clothes. I used to even buy a lot of my jars to can, when I first learned. It's so nice to have someone to talk to, that we have so much in common.

Well Happy Late Birthday, now I really am totally amazed. Your birthday April 2nd is my Dads, or I should say was my Dads. We used to laugh because he almost was born on April Fools Day. Ha Ha You too. So you're an Aries huh? Both of my folks were Areis, Mom birthday is 3-29. Wow, that must be why I hit it off right away with you Ed.

I had to laugh because my cellie was telling me about this guy she was getting ready to write, that wrote her from Jail Babes, and guess what? It's you. I told her you & I are writing also. Small world huh? What type of class will you be teaching in San Juans? Tell me more.

I can't express how happy your letters make me, your just so interesting and down to earth. I'll admit in the beginning I was totally against this whole idea of writing anyone. Still a little gun shy, I guess. But when my cellie was explaining to me that I had too much time left to not receive mail, and then the simple fact that I really do need help, well I decided to take a chance and as I've said before you are the only person who has answered my ad "excluding the pervert" He doesn't count. But I truely enjoy hearing from you and very much appreciate your sending me the stationary. Now I can write you more.

Ed if ever you win the lottery (smile) please keep me in mind. HaHa. Oh I have had a little good news.....My little portu job has gotten me an 8 cent an hour pay sbt. Yippee This last month I worked 87 hrs and made $6.72, hey it's a start huh? The only bummer with this is, they take out 22% for my restitution, if it ain't one thing its another. I just keep my chin up and hopes high that hopefully soon my ship will come in and life will be made just a little bit more easier or at least comfortable in here. Its bad enough just being here but my Lord it's a struggle when you don't have your needs. I learned real quick- though (THANK GOD) I'M A FAST LEARNER!! Yes Ill never borrow <u>ANYTHING,</u> again, this two for one pay back its highway robbery, worse than a loan shark and a lot more deadly. Yes I learned the hard way. Thank goodness I'm no longer a HIGH Maintenance female (smile) Just a little lady who made a bad choice and ended up in "The belly of the beast".

      Thats what I call this hell hole. Ok. I can't believe I just cried all over your shoulders. Thanks Ed for listening, I think I really needed to vent. Let me find a darn picture, I've got to have a decent one somewhere? The only one I can think of that I have right now is me in a wedding dress (oh boy) Now next month they are taking photos here, I'd wrote and asked my mom if she could send me some $. And now I feel terrible for asking her because shes barely making it on her SSI. But hopefully she'll be able to send me enough for a picture or two. Ill let you know, and I sure do thank you & appreciate the offer of you'll make me some copies. It all means so much.

      Well my friend let me run this to the box. Let me know how you really are. Tell me all about your new adventures and your teaching.
                  Waiting to hear from you soon
                          Always, Connie

P/S. You really are a great Bud

Letters from Prison

Author's Note:

Well, this honeymoon didn't last long. Her second letter and, although she's as subtle as Jennifer, she's already asking for money. Her poor old mom on SSI was a good touch, also. I guess I shouldn't have sent her the stationary.

May 15, 2001
Dear Ed,

Just a little note to say hello. I haven't heard from you for awhile so just thought I'd let you know, your always being thought of.

The weather is starting to get nice, so I'm sure your real busy. I hope lifes treating you Special because thats what you are to me, very special and I really enjoy our friendship.

I've been out to the hospital for a couple of weeks. My minor surgery, having a small cyst removed, turned into major surgery and then all kinds of complications from the medication (Great) just my luck. Thank God I've always been healthy because I don't ever want to see a doctor here, again. What a nightmare.

Ed, did I ever send you a visiting form? Please let me know. Someday it would be really nice to meet you in person. Well I guess I'll close I just really wanted to say hi.

Always thinking of you. Connie

Author's Note:

It must have taken me a while to send a response to her previous letter. It appears she might be a little worried her plea for money had put me off.

Letters from Prison

May 18, 2001

Dear Ed,

    Hello there, our mail must have crossed , that makes me feel good, at least we were both thinking of each other at the same time. You sound great as usual, and I appreciate so much that photo you sent of the Chetco River. I sure do miss Oregon, there are the most beautiful places I'd ever been to, right there. I've always pretty much tried not to live with a lot of regrets. But...Damn, I wish Id never left Brookings. And I seriously can't wait until the day I can return. I used to have a blast dancing at the Sporthaven, do they still have live bands?

    Yeah Ed, I guess we just got lucky with the stationary package..A new memo was just posted telling us after June 15th, we won't be allowed any more to be sent, only stamps or embossed envelopes. You know just one more thing to make life more difficult.

    I had to crack up at the part of your letter where you mentioned, Gail. Yes...she is my cellie, I have seven of them, unfortunately . But honest to God we don't discuss you or really too much of anything. We really don't have a lot in common. She is nice but just not someone I would hang around. So maybe you should just explain to me what ever it is you told her. "only" if you feel it necessary. Ed, all you have to go on is my word, I take pride in being who I am. I'm not out to cheat or lie about anything, and I do so much appreciate your friendship. All I ask is that we keep it between us. I'm not real big on a lot of the so called friendships in here. Truthfully I look at it like it's a concrete jungle and theirs a lot of snakes!! Oh let me switch back to the picture of the Chetco Yeah my Mom had mentioned something awhile back about the new dock and all of the new sights in Brookings and Harbor.

Now as to the money order, thats so sweet of you and I swear couldn't come at a better time. I've never stressed out so bad before, hell I guess I didn't even know what stress was ! Really thank you. You just make out a postal money order to me with my name & W# on it. Now they have a direct P.O. Box 94 that it goes to, but when you send it, do not put any letter or card, note or anything with it, that way it won't get returned and will be posted right away. You really are a good guy and I really do value your friendship.

I was laughing when you said Gail was someone you could get drunk and stupid with, I hear that (smile). To be honest the mood I'm in I wouldn't mind getting drunk & stupid too. Speaking of drinking, is Ken's Tavern still there in Brookings? Here's an old memory...do you remember the Green Door?

Hey the class your teaching sounds pretty cool ! Anything now days to save some $. Thats a good thing. Next month there taking photos here. I'm really gonna try to get to take one, hopefully I'll have a new updated picture to send you soon. If I have to, I'll even take one with a friend just so I can be in the picture.

Well I guess I've talked your ear off enough for today. You have a great day and know that your always being thought of.

From the bottom of my heart, I want to thank you again.

Hugs Always, Connie

Author's Note:

I know what you're thinking... after my previous experiences, why was I sending this woman money? What kind of idiot am I? Try to understand, I felt this was an investment in someone I might hire in the future. Okay, you're right. I was an idiot! I also thought it was tax deductible.

Connie mentions her cell mate, Gail, with whom I was also corresponding. This happened several times, as I had no way of knowing who was sharing a cell with whom. However, it was something I was careful to try to avoid in the future, as it can create major problems between cell mates.

June 5, 2001
Dear Ed,

Hello there my friend, I just received your most welcome letter. I love the picture as always. Aw the good life! EEEE HAAAA! Your letter explaining to me your reason behind writing women in prison, especially life/longtimers honest to God touched my heart.

You accually brought tears to my eyes. I can truely understand how your friend must have felt when her family turned their backs on her. Mine pretty much did that to me years ago, I guess I was really a major let down. After I divorced I got pretty wild & crazy, drinking a lot, truthfully nothing anymore than everyone else was doing, but I guess no one expected it coming from me. I never really speak on my past much Ed, because its such a done deal. But I feel pretty comfortable with you and your so down to earth, I like that. Anyways it amazes me by watching the different lives around here (prison) I mean other races, seriously such as Mexican & blacks always have their familys support. Especially the blacks, its amazing man. I mean speaking by my own experience and opinion of course   It honestly makes me sick how quick white familys are to turn their backs. Guess my folks got burnt out way before I ever had a chance (smile) because my older brother & sister had really put them through it.   Now such is my case when I need someone the most they're all passed away, except my Mom and she's sure not in any position to help me in any way.
You see as I explained before my Moms 72 yrs old, real sick

Letters from Prison

and heres something I never mention, she's an alcklic. Anyways since you shared with me I thought I'd share my story with you. Your really a special guy and have an incredible big heart. Your intelligent and I'm sure you have the ability to tell who's real and who isn't.

Oh before I forget always as soon as I received your letters I answer them, maybe we just crossed in the mail?? Because you asked me about your May 10th letter, I could have swore I answered it. The mail here is really slow. Believe me I am very grateful for your letters and I look so forward to receiving them. Your friend said it right "your letters are my salvation." My cellies all receive so much mail, it does feel great when I hear my name called at mail call. Thank you so much for being who you are. I pretty much just do my little day to day job in here. Mind my own business. This place here is no joke. I've seen it all !! Literally . I'm one of those people who seem to attrack crazy people? There are some real weird ones walking around in here 2 cans shy of a six pack, and don't cha know they always come & talk to me. Maybe a lot of that has to do with my job is right here in my housing unit so I'm subjected to being around em all. But if I had my way I'd be up the Chetco River surrounded by no one but the fresh air & the water. I'm more of a dog person than a people person. Does that make sense? In here if your not sharp, these snakes will chew you up & spit you out. It's a concrete jungle, for real.

Well Ed, I just want to say, thanks again for being who you are and being my friend. Oh by the way...I'm feeling much better, guess it will take more than this sorry states witch doctor to do me in .

Take care

Big Hugs Connie

Letters from Prison

Author's Note:

At this point, I felt Connie was a person who could become part of my future plans for the sports bar. Having seen a picture taken at the prison, I knew she was attractive and her letters tell me she is bright enough to handle the job and would make a good employee.

June 11, 2001
Dear Ed,

    Hi just received your letter, and I love the seals !! They're so cute I cut the picture off your letter & hung it up. Yep, I sure do know Cresent City. I've heard that its changed so much, since they built the prison. I met a girl in here that was from Smith River, and she was telling me how big it all is now. I really agree with your concept. I mean if more people in this world would look at ex-con's like you do, I bet the statistics of the majority of people coming right back, wouldn't !! I mean if they are just given a chance. So many are so quick to judge, instead of getting to know a person and not catagorize them. I really like your out look on the whole subject. Ed, even in here I've been told many times that I have a really good attitude   considering. And hell no (smile) I don't want to be here, and sure don't like scrubbing the cops toliet (literally) but...hey it's my job and things could always be worse.

    Thats really too bad about your daughter's boyfriend, that really sucks and really does go to show that it's extremely difficult for an ex-convict.

    Hey I <u>really</u> like the idea of a Sports Bar & Grill, Hmph! with a sailing theme. That would really be different. I'd sure work there and now your right about the world being politically correct. I'll be the first to admit (smile) I sure wouldn't mind someone patting me on the butt, especially right about now   but on a serious note, yeah I

Letters from Prison

think a female whos done some time would be more apt to deal with the customers. Considering being in here your sexually harassed a lot. Or at least I have been. I remember once my boss telling me to go count some carts of food in the cooler. (Yeah Right) Well needless to say he thought he was going toss me up   in the friggen cooler. Come on now, what a jerk. And then theres been you know everything from threats to promises, etc etc. So yes I do believe that a woman whos done some time could handle herself.

Now that was just a couple of stories about the men here, that doesn't even begin to cover the stories about the women   . Oh yeah. All about kicking their ass (smile) yep I think they would take me serious. I'm not very big but believe me, I can hold my own. Ed did I ever send you a picture? I swear I can't remember. Let me know. I'm sure I can find some ugly ole photo, somewhere   He Hee. Well I guess you sent me this pretty stationary right on time, because now they're not allowing us to get it anymore. Nope we have to buy paper now!!

Well Ed, guess Ill run this to the box, I think we have a letter crossed in the mail? I really enjoy talking to you. Your one helluva guy.

That was so cute "I could trust you with anything" except the space between my...nose & toes!   I'm still laughing over that one. I can't wait to hear from you again. Seriously Ed, thanks for being a friend. Someday were gonna paint the town.

Take Care

Your Friend Always, Connie

Author's Note:

As you can see, I'd confided in Connie my real reason for writing. I got the impression she was excited at the prospect of having a potential job when she got out. Now

Letters from Prison

I had to tell her I was a married man and this was strictly business.

June 11, 2001
Dear Ed,

Oh my God ... I'm in love! Your bike is beautiful, I'd love to be flying down the highway with the wind in my face. Every now & then, like if I'm out on the yard, I'll get to hear off in the distance, a harley. Hey last night I got your letter really late because you put the wrong housing. So tell me some of your stories about things you do & see driving truck.

You mentioned Riverside, thats where I lived for awhile, Riverside & Moreno Valley back before it was called Moreno Valley. It used to be Sunnymead and was pretty much a little biker neighborhood. I loved it . Always had a secret admiration for rugged men and Harleys.

You & I have crossed letters in the mail, because this one is exactly what we talked about in one other letter. It's all good! Guess I enjoy receiving your mail so much, that a second dose of seeing what a helluva guy you are made my day, again. Don't forget now that I still look damn good in a mini skirt & halter top (smile) so I most definately want a job at your club.

I hear what your saying about the other races Ill admit I'm so sick of hearing that bullshit crying racism in here. That gets old quick. Oh before I forget Ed, I never did receive the money order, please don't take me wrong, I'm just worried that this place misplaced it?? Let me know. Yep I sure would rather be around a dog than a person or people, much more loyal, protective either they like you or they don't, no false pretences. Oh I'm sticking in a photo, not a good one but its all I've got for now. Truthfully the one in Jail Babes is terrible too. But at least this way you can see a little bit of what I look like.

Letters from Prison

So you're a closet pervert huh ? Well I hear that "wink."

There's a lot of stories from in here, a lot not worth telling. I'll be honest I've never seen so many ugly people all in one place as I have in here. And not just on the outside. It blew my mind when I first came here because they are seriously women who not only look like men, but righteously act like em. Now my philosiphy is...if your gonna be with a woman, why not be with a pretty one! Go ahead my lil closet pervert, ask me. I know your dieing too (smile)

Tell me more about your bike, I've been sitting looking at Easyrider, oh my God I saw the biggest pair of titties I've ever seen in my life. I'm talking ridiculously huge. HUGE. Don't ask me why but my spirits have been like way lifted. I just decided to stop trippin and be my usual ole self, staying bubbly & laughing off everything. It beats the hell outta crying. Things will get greater later, so Im told. Today is my day off, from my majorly important corporate job   Wink. So I've scrubbed & cleaned, even waxed my floor. Hey Sugga, even concrete looks pretty waxed !! Yes I'm a clean freak! Yikes.

Ed I don't think you've ever told me what kind of music you like? This meaning music is something I can't live without, at least not in here.

Well I'm just babbling on & on, makin no sense so I guess Ill bring this to a close. Can't wait to hear from you again.

If your ever down this way, I'd sure like for you to come for a visit. Want me to send you a form?

 Have a Great Day
 Hugs & Kisses Connie

Author's Note:

I found myself drawn to this woman, both as a

potential employee and as an individual. I was a bit afraid she might be reading more into my letters than I intended and my next one clarified my marital status and domestic happiness.

June 24, 2001
Hi Ed,

Just a lil thank you note   I'm at work and this pen sucks   I just received the money order. It sure came right on time, now that its posted Ill be able to shop July's shop And well considering July 15th is my birthday well Ill feel like its my present!! Your generous-heart means so much to me. I'm very appreciative.

How's everything going with you? I still can't get over your bike. I love it. I'm sorry this has to literally be a note (smile) But I've got to get busy before the coppers get me.

Thanks from the bottom of my heart.

Always Connie

Author's Note:

The fact that she took the time to write this thank you note convinced me even more that she could be a future employee.

June 28, 2001
Ed,

Hi there honey - got ahold of this cute paper and just had to send it to you. Along with the damn photo, that I forgot to put in your last letter.

How's life treating you?   Heard any new jokes lately? As for me hey I'm doing fine, just staying busy. I enjoy my lil job, I've even taken on a lil side job with pay for ten bucks a month I've been washing & ironing a dames !! laundry. Truthfully it sucks   but its honest.

> *I've sent away for some courses by mail. If I qualify maybe Ill be able to earn some college credits and learn something that will benifit me out there someday. Ill let ya know, how it turns out Sure hope you can read this geez it's 200 AM, I just couldn't sleep. My God 3 of my cellies are snoring soooo loud. Real lady like huh? Wish I had a tape recorder   Ha Ha.*
>
> *Its finally cooled off a little bit here. Thank God, I just knew I was in the pits of hell a couple weeks ago 107° Yuk.*
>
> *Well my friend, guess I'll go try it again. Sleep has to come eventually (I Hope) Oh also here's a visiting form so in case your ever down this way. Just thinking of how Special you are. Thanks for being you!*
>
> > *Big Hugs*
> > *Always Connie*

Author's Note:

I laughed at the 2:00 a.m. insight, closing my eyes and visualizing the scene she so briefly described. Not quite the sleep-overs I remembered as a child.

> *July 11, 2001*
> *Ed,*
> *Hello Sugga -*
>
> *Just received your letter, so you've been camping huh? Then sailing too, okay now thats enough, yer killin me (smile)*
>
> *I laughed when you said, how your Dad was "barking" out orders for 8 days. Isn't that how they are, thats what makes em so special. I know my Dad tried to act so tuff and mean but my whole life I knew he was "my marshmellow".*

Letters from Prison

Hey don't worry about the mail mix up, it's all straight now, so I'll get it on time. I wrote you and thanked you for the m.o., wow, whats really going on? Didn't you receive my thank you note? By now surely you've received the photo I sent. Yes my Boo Boo, I did leave it laying on my bed when I mailed your letter, but ... I did send a back up note & sent the picture. No silly I did not send it to the pervert   Please let me know ASAP "if" you have ever received the photo & thank you note. This really has me trippin. Thank you for the photo of you, even if it is 1992, cut it out "old & fat" no your not, I think a man of your caliber is just like fine wine, only gets better with age

I am so sincerly sorry to hear about you & the IRS. That Sucks!! Well darlin' if I was out, I'd help you out & write a check.....JUST Kidding   Seriously I'm trying to cheer you up. I don't want to sound like a commie or something, but I really can't stand our government. They're whole concept is schiety (sp?) Put your gloves on Ed & fight em. Now I'm livid (wife) oh thats it!! Just when I thought I'd get cha to merry me. Auk!! O' Well, Ill be the other woman (smile) Wish I was there to at least give you that good lay you want, now thats one for sure thing, I know I can do. Now as for me having any fun lately with a cellie, in the dark   Nope...NADA, I haven't had a pretty cellie for ages. I swear I always seem to get either the nuts or the one's with an identify crisis. Why Me?   I 100% identify with what your saying about Friends you can love, not lover's that you have to try to be friends with. Hell yes I understand.

ooh Flash bulletin, I might as well break this to you gently... I certainly don't have a big set of tittles, sorry babes, but their pretty and believe me I have something else you can bury your face in. Wink. I don't think you'd be disappointed. And I'm told a real nice ass too!!

> *How long do you think its gonna take until your Harley touches down? Okay (smile) now you really did it, I'm in <u>love</u>. Bob Sagar, now thats music night moves, Accompany ME, turn the page like a Rock, Yeah I love Sagar too.*
>
> *Ill go see the counselor and see what she says, Ill let you know. In the mean time here's a form.*
>
> *Lets get this party started*
> > *Forever Your Friend Connie*
>
> *Write soon. I adore your letters.*

Author's Note:

Well, I guess finding out I was married didn't curb her enthusiasm. As to various references in this and other letters, I often joked with the women I wrote to, commenting on the stereotypical prison characters and sex scenes on television and in the movies.

Her disappointment regarding the Harley was a result of my explaining to her I'd had to cancel my order for the new bike, given the financial demands of battling the IRS.

> *July 28, 2001*
> *Dear Ed,*
> *Hello Darling'*
>
> *Just received your most welcome letter, matter of fact I was seriously stalking the mail handlers wondering where you were! Ok now all of this torture is just a bit much, (smile) Your p/u and 5th wheel are beautiful. You sure do have some nice toys.*
>
> *Speaking of government issues; IR-f-igs etc etc. Please allow me to run this by you, hopefully you can give me some good solid advise. Last Friday I received legal*

mail and was informed by my deceased husbands "Employee Benefit Dept". that I am entitled to his fully vested IRA. Its most definitely a large amount of money. Now this investment firm thats been handling his $, is asking me what I'd like to do. OH GOD!! They've sent me all kinds of materials on Prospectus, books on Stock Funds Inc. Templet on Institutional Funds -Inc. Stock Fund, Balanced Fund, Income Fund Small Companies, Large Companies. HELP. I have zero knowledge about <u>any</u> of this. The first thing I thought was pull the $ from them have it sent here, take like a 30% loss to the friggen government, and be happy content, be able to shop canteen have all of the things I so desperately want & need in here. Yes instant gratification!!! But then I layed awake all night trippen on what a waste. Why not get some for myself, here & now, but leave the rest to make $. I'm <u>so</u> confused, I don't know the right thing to do. All of this is "Greek" to me. All I know is I knew in my heart something would come through, that I hadn't suffered like this for nothing. Meaning I believe when you bottom out, have to humble yourself, go without etc. that eventually you will see your blessings. Ed, I'm a good person and just want to do whats best for me in the long run. Any advice will be welcome. I feel very close to you too, your so down to earth and I trust you. Ill admit for me thats hard considering everything thats happened in my life.

  Anyways I'm at work thats why I didn't write you on the pretty blue paper, sorry hon, yer stuck with this ole ugly white paper. The question about your friend Gail, no comment. My Daddy always taught me if I didn't have sumthang nice to say, keep my big mouth shut!! Don't take me wrong, she's nice just not someone I wish to be around.

  Someday bucko I'm gonna take you up on that hair parting, sweat on my face, knee nibbling escapade. Yep sure will!! I haven't got in yet to the counselor, she's never around, maybe you could call her. Her name is Mrs. Atkins.

> *Yes I can use the phone, Id love to give you a call. Ill try like hell to remember the 1-800-Collect (yeah right). I've gotta run, take care of yourself & <u>PLEASE</u> write back soon and give me some advice.*
>
> *I'm So Confused. How was Seattle?*
>
> *Always Connie*

Author's Note:

I'm going to stand on the fifth, regarding some of her closing comments. She and I did a great deal of teasing, as you can see, and I gave as good as I got.

In response to Connie's concerns about the investments, I suggested she put 75% of her money in the S&P 500, 20% in a higher risk fund and take 5% and blow it on herself.

Unfortunately, this is the last letter I received from Connie. Perhaps her windfall made a difference in her situation. For whatever reason, she chose not to write me again. I hope she's well. She seemed to be a decent person who had made some bad choices in her life. I would have hired her to work for me. I felt she would have been a loyal employee.

Shannon

Arizona State Prison Complex

Goodyear, AZ

March 27, 2001
Daniel

  Hi ~~Daniel~~ or Ed I'm sorry!! It's great to meet you I have to tell you I don't have any pen pals right now so getting a letter from you made my day. I get mail from my friends here but it's nice to meet someone new. I wish we could have met under different circumstances but I guess if it weren't for these circumstances we would not have met huh. For the kind of person I am I never thought I would end up here. I got a lot more time in here than some people who did things really wrong like drugs and theft etc but I guess God put me here for this long for a reason. I'm not a real religious person but I feel I could be doing a lot better things if I was out ! Ha Ha What I mean is I love to be there and help people too as you being there for people in here I think it is awesome, I'm sure you being so caring means a lot to a lot of people. You seem really nice. I work during the day on the farm crew boxing vegetables like broccolli and cabbage for places like the food banks, churches, homeless people basically. Not exactly my life long career dream and MADD gets all my income (Mothers against Drunk Drivers) so I stay on this crew because it's my way of helping people that makes me feel good. You know what? D.O.C is suposed to get a Rubbermaid job for us

> inmates but I don't know whats going on with that. What I'm really worried about is what and where I'll be working when I get out, I mean bartending is all I really know and I'm sure it won't be easy finding a job with my record now, but I guess I'll deal with it when I get out. You seem so easy going, beautiful picture, is that in Oregon? Do you like traveling every where? I haven't been to many places in my life. I was born in Tucson and this is as far as I got but one day would love to see a lot of other places. Unfortunately when I get out I will have probation to deal with so that will hold me back for a while, but a promise to myself I will see more of this world before I die. Well I'd love to hear from you again, I hope I didn't babble to much on my 1st letter, I'm just not good at this, just wanted to tell you a little about me. Take care of yourself Daniel or Ed and don't have to much fun !!
>
> *Hey thanks for the stamps.*
>
> *Bye for now Shannon*
>
> *Hey is your name Daniel or Ed? ! You make me laugh, I'm writing you picturing Ed and then I read the envelope and it says Daniel anyway that's why I crossed out your name at the beginning of this letter.*
>
> *PS - Yes the littlest things amuse me. Ha Ha Sorry this took so long, my letter got returned, your numbers to your address are different from the address on the envelope. I hope you get this letter*

Author's Note:

    I'd written Shannon because her bio stated she'd been a bartender. After reviewing her record, I learned she'd been convicted of drunk driving and I was pretty sure no parole officer would allow her to work in a job selling alcohol. However, I continued to write to her, in the event this wasn't the case.

April 07, 2001

Hi Ed, How's it going? Me, I'm hanging in there. It was nice to hear from you again. I'm glad you finally got my letter. Little Ed huh? I think Its kinda cute. It sounds like your family and you are close, that is so awesome Nice picture, but sorry you don't look like a Tough trucker to me, you look kind of cuddly, at least that's what I saw, and no I'm not flirting with you, you seem like a very nice, buff man to me (little Ed) !! I'm sorry I'm just teasing with you. Your letter gave me the impression you can handle it and I like to be silly sometimes.

Speaking of being silly get this, we were digging trenches around the farm today and there is this one girl who is very macho and thought she can do just about anything, well she kept talking about how she had these kind of trenches at home she used to jump over all the time, well these are pretty wide trenches so I dared her to jump it. I didn't think she would but she did, and broke her ankle in 2 places. Stupid huh! I forgot how daring I was when I was her age. UGGG! Does that mean I'm getting old? Anyway I'm not one to gossip about others. I just wanted to share one of my interesting moments in my stay here.

Well I guess I can say the time is going by fast for me, I've been down a year and have 2.9 left so It will be over before I know it. Thanks for writing back, and back to you ---as long as you want to write to me, I love to share my experiences with you, in and out of here K? K! Anyway if we do continue writing I would like to send you another picture of me as well but the only thing is I only have one set so if I sent you one you would have to promise to make a copy of it and send it back . Sorry but that's all I have so if you wanted to do that just let me know if not that's ok too, just that picture in that ad is from Christmas a couple years ago, it's all I had at the time.

> *Anyway it was nice talking to you again Ed, be careful out there and write back when you can*
> *Bye for now Shannon*

Author's Note:

    I sent Shannon copies of the photo, as she requested. It seemed a simple thing to do. Based on her initial letters, I liked her sense of humor and felt if something could be worked out, given her record and the business I was opening, she would be a good addition to the sport bar and restaurant.

> *April 13, 2001*
>
> **May the promise of this holy time of year fill**
> **Your world with blessings and fill your heart with**
> **The abundant hope and joy that only Jesus gives.**
>
> Ed,
>
>   *I just wanted to wish you a very Happy Easter. Kind of a corny card but it's all they had to offer. So with the sincere words from this card, have a great day.!!*

Author's Note:

    At this point, I was corresponding with several inmates, but this was the first time I found myself feeling sorry for one of them. I realized that whatever happened, when Shannon was driving drunk, had to have been pretty heinous, given the lengthy sentence she got. Still, it saddened me to realize that, in her sober state of mind, she really didn't belong where she was. I could only hope that, after Shannon served her time, she never picked up a drink again.

Letters from Prison

April 18, 2001
Ed,

Hello my friend. Well by the time you get this letter Easter will be over. Did you get my card? Easter is one of my favorite holidays. Usually I'd go and borrow someones kids for the day and spoil them rotten, along with me. I'm still such a child or at least like to act like it once in a while. I hope your Easter was fun.

God Ed you really see some beautiful places. I've been to San Diego once. Awesome, I love the ocean and the beach, as you'll be able to see in these pictures. Sorry all of them I have sunglasses on. I guess it was a bright day! Ha Ha But I am trying to get others as well. I'll send you one without my sunglasses to asure you I'm not crosseyed.!! I'm also inclosing a picture of my best friend I would like you to meet. This guy is my world. He's just waiting until I get out so we can kick it again. I really miss him. I used to take him tubing down the Salt River with me all the time. He evan had his own tube. I would tell him right before the rapids hit, "Get on your own tube" and he would. Great dog! Until you go to punish him for something and he gives me my additude. Anyway Ed you don't have to keep a picture if you don't want. I just wanted you to get to know <u>me</u> a little better since we've became friends. Please, please send them back when you can. They are my only ones for now.

Thanks.

I loved the story about your ditch incident. I'm sorry but you made me laugh. I'm sure it wasn't funny then, but we can laugh now right? !! I love bikes, I evan know how to drive one, One down three up right? Gears Ed, I'm talking about Gears! I'm just playing Ha Ha. You know it sure is nice you got a good sense of humor, lifes to short for cranky people huh! Ok I'll go for now. Write back when you can, Don't have to much fun and I'll talk to you soon.

Take care, Shannon

Letters from Prison

Author's Note:

I continued to be convinced Shannon was a good person, who'd made a terrible mistake. If we could work out the details, she was at the top of my list of people I'd like to hire.

May 8, 2001
Hi, Ed,

Hey Buddy, How are things going? Your such a busy man, that's nice of you to find the time to drop a line in between states. Your everywhere all the time. It sounds like you have a awesome time. You be safe out there K. Thank you so much for the copys they came in handy, I have to give a picture to get a picture. No really it's just that a lot of us girls like to get pictures of each other to take home with them to remember the cool people and the good things that come out of a bad situation, Unfortunately that's the only pictures I have but I have a few friends leaving this month so that's what I meant by they came in handy.

Anyway.....

Nice truck, I had a friend that had one just like it, I loved to drive it. It's so big (at least it was for me) talk about being King of the road. Ha Ha. When I can finally get my license back I would like to get a jeep, or another convertable, oh, I can't wait until this is all over with, but the time is going by pretty fast, I went from 3.9 to 2.8. I just have to keep reminding myself this isn't forever. Well I'll be moving soon, but I don't know when so when you write just use the same address and I'll let you know when the change comes. Hey Ed are you ok with writing me? I mean I don't ever want it to be a hassle for you, having a Pen-Pal is supposed to be fun I just don't ever want you to feel stuck if you know what I mean. if you ever can't write just let me know I'll understand, and I'll always be your friend.

> *I just wanted you to know that K? K. I'll go for now. Please take care and have lots of fun!*
>
> *Friends Forever, Me*

May 22, 2001
Ed,

    I didn't mean for you to take my question wrong. I just wanted you to know that I'm ok. And if you couldn't write It's ok. I really like writing to you so I'm glad that situation is over with Ha Ha! Sorry Silly.

    Anyway - Thanks for the pictures you send me I keep them all as if I was there too and hope one day to really see it for myself. It sounds like every time you take your boat out with people. every time is a new exsperience. No matter how many times you've done it, you've got to have a great time, and meeting different people all the time is awesome. I'm such a people person I know I would enjoy it.

    You know, I think buying a bar and grill is a great Idea, if it's in a good location and you know what your doing you can't go wrong and enjoy doing it and if I could I would almost beg you to let me be part of it and I know I would do you proud. But they won't let me work anywhere, where alcohol is even dispensed while I'm on probation. But I say for you, go for it. I just know it would work. But Ed please do me a favor. Your right when you say It's going to be hard for me to get a job when I get out because what I do so well I can't do, so if you ever come up with any Ideas for me, let me know. I'm so worried about what kind of career I'm going to be able to get into especially having a felony record. Some people won't mind since it's for Duis but a lot of people will frown on it. But keep in mind whatever you may come up with, I'm a fast learner, with a good additude. Thank you.

> *That would have been nice to meet you in person, and I haven't had a visit in a while, it would have been nice to see a friendly smile. I will get you a visitation application so if the occasion ever occurs again I won't miss out. But I will be moving in about 2 weeks to Santa Maria but I don't know what cell on the address so I'll wait to send it until I have all the info. Since you'll need it for your info K.*
>
> *It was real nice hearing from you again. Keep in touch. And let me know what you think. Until then take care of yourself and be careful - it's a jungle out there.*
>
> *Ha Ha   Bye for now -- Me*

Author's Note:

This letter made me realize how frightening it must be for this woman to recognize the very thing she can do to make a decent living is prohibited as an option. I'm not discounting what she did, just commenting on understanding how terrible it must be to not know what you're going to do, how you're going to support yourself, when you get out of prison.

> *June 5, 2001*
> *Ed,*
>
> *Hey Ed. Nice to hear from you again. Nice ride you got there. I think when I finally get my licence back I might want to get me a motorcycle, not only because there cool but because you don't often see women on bikes but I think it's kind of sexy and I love to feel the fresh air on my face. I don't remember if I told you but I used to have a convertable. Now I would like to be different. I'm sorry but I had to laugh at your story about the girl in the store. We have some of those kind here, they act like there to good to*

Letters from Prison

be in a place like this. Wow what a big slap in the face it must have been when there parents couldn't buy there way out of this situation. Anyway I would have loved to see the expression on that girls face when you said that - Good for you!! Boy I sure wish I could work at your bar and grill. I understand what you mean about the B.S. that would come of being a boss and finding the "right" people to employ. I am exactly what you would be looking for, Well I would have to be, bartending for 5yrs, you need personality for money (always keep them coming back) and additude for respect. God you would think for as much time as they gave me they wouldn't be so hard on me when I get out, I mean how much rehabilitation does one need, if 4 yrs in prison doesn't cure you, nothing will. Limo Service sounds awesome too. Whatever you decide to do, I can tell you will be a awesome boss - I'm moving next Monday so as soon as I get there I will send a visitation form. I know I still have a while Ed but do you think I could make it out there in Oregon if I decided to start over there? Just a question, like I said I realize I still have some time but I still think about what's best for my future everyday. Hey, thanks for sharing your thoughts and your dreams with me, It always gives me a positive outlook on what I would really like to do. If you run into anymore snobs just slap her and tell her "GET OVER IT' just kidding but don't you feel like doing it sometimes?

    Take care Ed

               With love Shannon

Author's Note:

    It saddens me to say that, after her move from this facility, I never regained contact with Shannon. I hope she picks up a copy of this book out of curiosity and recognizes her letters and tries to get in contact. I would do what I can to help her assimilate back into society. Hopefully, in time, I can provide jobs for the Shannon's of the world.

Kimberly

C.R.C. Prison

Norco, CA

March 29, 2001

Hello Ed

I am glad you wrote me and I'd be happy to write you! And get to know you "Better." And on top of everything I would love to have you as my new friend if not more someday. But I'll make this letter a one pager because it takes so long to get to me. I am in a new unit 406-5B. But I sure hope this doesn't come back. You have put down two PO Boxes   Ok. I can tell you I am a "Brat" but a fun one. So this place is a drug program and thats what Im in 6 days a week with no-pay. But I am learning a lot about my-self OK, and it did safe my life. I would love to have a visit from you some day to. But I'll send it off my next letter to make sure this one does make it to you   ok. Did you have to pay Jail Babes for the "Info" for me? I was wondering about that, will you please tell me how they work that Info.

Sorry for the messy letter, but Im tired ok. To tell you the truth I don't know a thing about them. But I wanted to meet new people and good real one's at that. Do you flipp through Jail Babes offen or what!! You will come to find out I am a "Smart Ass" I'll be laughing the hole time being one. And things that will make me smile and laugh I want a part of. Id sure be happy if I know I am makeing some one else smile. If you like to spoil me? My arm's are wide open   ...

> *Being locked-up isn't easy your wright. But it sure is going fast and most defintley getting shorter every day.*
>
> *HMMM You'll figure it out wont you on why you had to write me with a close release date. Your cute an have made me smile from ear to ear. By the way they typed up my age wrong? I am 55 year's old Hee Hee !! "Not" Quack. My age is really 35 Born 9-13-65 Vrigo? That's the truth. I can deal with the not necessarily not the soul mate part right now. But you never know who will end up as your soul-mate nowadays. But like I said I would love to meet your Mug in Real life. But I'll wait to hear back from you first. Hay make your letter smell good so I can remember what a man smell's like   . But this girl need's some sleep, Because brain is not working for me.*
>
> *Love Your New Friend Kimberly*

Author's Note:

When I first saw this woman's photo, it screamed sassy and this letter did nothing to change my first impression. The only problem was her release date was sooner than my target date.

I was hopeful that, after her release, we could stay in touch and she could stay out of trouble until I got my project launched.

> *April 23, 2001*
>
> *Hello Mr. Ed III*
>
> *Sorry for my spelling I'am way off with it an real messy. SoRRy The classes have me writing a lot right now and the hand hurts.*
>
> *Sorry I have been sitting on my ass and not writing right back. But the truth is I have been bussy or lets say this*

place has me running my ass off. I've put myself in this Peer Ed Training that lasts one more week. Im learning all about Health care and how to speak to the new weman comeing in. Its all right to know more, But theres a lot more then I thought to remember. So my brain is on full and its got more to go . But I guess thats why Iam here in this Waldan House Program. Love the pictures you printed out, I sure would love to be on that Boat. But the last time I was on one was when I was 14 and puked my brains out !! I did'nt have fun and to top it off, I grow up on the beach. As you can see it did no good. So you we're a Big Wise Ass - With the big printout adderss. "I like" Hee Hee. So here are tow visiting forms just in case you screw up on one HaHa Boy the girls here are crazey or the one's that are coming in are to yong and just need a good ass Kickin

So you think every one born after 1950 are relay'ed to drugs. You could be right. Thanks about being right up front when you had done and stoped doing dope. Its nice to know that theres living poof HaHa!! Yes I am starting to be a wise ass. But Thank You for being on the real side. To tell you the truth we could all do with out drugs. It sure has not got me any where in the past, It just put a lot of money in my pokit. But where is all that money now, it went all to lawer's and the state just takes every thing and anything and left me broke and now in a drug program. But Ed it most likley safe'd my life. Ed don't worry about your gut to no knee's Hee Hee just kiddying. Its your personalty that is on hit. You're a nice guy right !! And have kick'ed drug's at one time.!! Thank you for telling me how the Jail Baby things work. So they make 7 doller's off me and don't even give me any, not that I Care. But they sure didn't say they charged. Made me laugh thinking of it. Some people will make there money anyway they can or what.

> *PS Well you would want to get some after I have, its been a hole year of being lock'ed up and I have forgottan what a man smells like ok. By the way thank's once again for the really Big print out of the adderss? I want one every time Ha Ha? More coming you way Big Guy! All be waitting ok?*
>
> *Kimberly*

Author's Note:

As you can see, Kimberly was fairly upbeat, but she couldn't spell to save her soul. If she worked for me, she'd be waiting tables a long, long time. The customers would love her, though.

> *May 29, 2001*
> *Hello Ed III*
>
> *So how's Mr, Ed doing today. So excues me for the delay on writeing back. But you can say I got lazey and all my free time I lay'ed around. And that's all I have done, just sleep'ed it all away. But here I sit in class now. And for some reason I can get a whole lot of writing done in class. We are just going over the same thing we did 5 months ago. My body is doing fine. So you like being on the road a lot, Its just not a job for you. But its nice to have work in your life that you like or love to do in this life time.*
>
> *So a trip to Hawaii then San Fran would have been my pick? But thank's for asking, But I am all tied up at this time and can not make it! Quack" Ha Ha. I wish it was that way. !! But it was nice to pretend that I had to say no to something like I was free out there ok. But yea for me! My paper work goes out next month to a new program on the streets, and that's a must in order to leave here. But the truth is I want to go to a program from here to get my feet on*

Letters from Prison

the ground in San Diego since I am on my own and no one to help me in that way at all. But bottom line 4 more months tops and Im out of here and start'ed on getting my life together right. So you say you write a whole lot of girl's in prison? Well that's nice !! I am happy for you. But Im going to ask, why not get to know weman out there that are free all ready. And the good part about how you can tell when a girl is working you !! Ha Ha Good one. So can you send me some money 30.00 would be nice Ha Ha Hee "<u>Quack</u>"..But on the real side of who your writing and your secerts. Ed you don't have to tell me anything when your ready or you feel like telling me. And if I ask you something just tell me the truth and tell me not now or your not ready to say anything. But you seem to be all right with your self, and what you like and don't like.!! AND thats alright in my book and I do like that in a man!! Yea for you!! Just scored one. Hee Hee And thank you for shareing you story about you and your friend and how you met her on the road and she's a friend for the long hall. And if its too much trouble getting somthing from a doctor for visiting, Don't trip. I just may be out there by that time. !! Hee Hee But the good side of that is we can visit out there if you don't make it because of the steel in your arm. But if you can make it still I want it ok. So I have something to tell you befor I close this letter and send it off to you.

So here is somthing to make you smile or laugh? If a fly lands in the beer of a normal drinker, He will order a new beer. If a fly lands in the beer of a problem drinker, He will shoo away the fly and drink the beer. If a fly lands in the beer an ahcoholic, He will pick it up the fly, Shake it! And shout "Spit it out, Spit it out! The power behind me is greater than the problem in front of me. If you don't want to slip, stay out of slippery places. Ha Ha. So its back to class for me and all be waitting to hear from you once again ok. The Brat Kimberly,

"Always Here for Now" Me

Letters from Prison

Author's Note:

Kimberly's upbeat attitude and the tone of her letters continued to make me feel she'd be an asset in the bar and restaurant business.

April 15, 2001

Hello Ed

Just want'ed to drop this card your way because in some way it reminds me of what little I know of you. But I also wanted to say "Hi" because I was thinking of you. By the way I show'ed your picture's off to a few ladys. !! Yea they be jealous but I got the letter from you, you for me. Hay when are let's say when I write my next letter to you Im going to ask you to print up or find some things off the Innet for my classes I'll be teaching on health care stuff ok. But just a Big Worm Smile and a card your way? Just becaues don't need a reason. I want to know more of you

More comeing From Me: Kimberly

June 22, 2001

Hi Ed

Well just another day closer to the gate opening for me anyway you look at it. "Yea" for me . Nice bike, To bad you only use it once in awhile. Hey don't work your self to death now. We most think of are health - right. !!

Boy this place is getting to me Ed and I hope its just for today ok. Its not even 8:00 am yet and I feel like this! Thanks for listening to me. And I know this will pass to all in a good day's work. But let me tell you that the house is in trouble and we all have to pay for it, and they don't want us going out on the yard unless we are program no phone they don't even want us to write letters or shop and stay on are

Letters from Prison

> bed's because a few girls in Walden House were breaking the rule's. Well we are still CDC state property and they cant stop all of that stuff in prison I can do this what ever they want, But they would want to think twice about what they are doing with over 200 girls in just are program alone in prison not good. But we will see. Now I feel better that I got to whine.! Sure all work for you in your sports Bar, that's good money. But I will not take off my cloths OK. By the way the guy you said had a hard time getting a job or holding one was full of shit. I have had no problem finding one and I have been on parole for some years. But I have to write a 1000 words befor bed time on haveing the last word.
>   More coming your way
>   Alway's here for now Kimberly

Author's Note:

Kimberly was released shortly after this and we've corresponded outside this forum. This is, however, "Letters from Prison," so the rest of her letters will remain private. You'll be happy to know her spelling is improving.

Nicole
Oregon Department of Corrections
Portland, OR

April 5, 2001
Dear Ed,

Hi there! I apologize for the delay in my response to your letter. I was transferred to a different facility on March 1st. Hey, at least they forwarded my mail, right?

You are right, it is not easy being locked up. Mail seems to make it better and in an effort to find pen-pals (who were not inmates), I decided to post on jail babes. It was great to get your letter - Thanks! You made my day!

It was great that you included a photo - I love it! That was a beautiful day sailing I bet! I've only been sailing once, just as a passenger. It was wonderful. I love boats in general and water activities as well. I don't know how to water ski though (unless it's frozen   )

I chose to write you partly because you said you are a good friend. That is hard to find these days!

In these last years since I left the US Coast Guard, I don't know that I've met a true one. I am a positive person and I keep looking because I know there are some to be found. I've probably been looking in the wrong places.

Anyway I could use a friend right now. My mom is terminal with bone cancer and I do not think she will be alive to see my release from prison. I used to confide in her, but it would only burden her now.

> *I am a <u>very</u> happy person and despite all that is going on, smile every day! So please don't think I won't be <u>fun</u> to write !*
>
> *If you ever want to see something funny take me golfing. I tried once at the VA in Roseburg and averaged about 15 strokes per hole - . I had a blast though.*
>
> *Well, I should get this out so you know I got your letter! It was nice to meet you! I hope to hear from you soon.*
>
> *Always, Nicole*

Author's Note:

Nicole seemed to be just what I was looking for. She'd been in the Coast Guard, so she must be somewhat intelligent, have some discipline. Also, having worked in a field dominated by men, I figured she'd have a pretty thick skin.

> *April 20, 2001*
> *Dear Ed,*
>
> *I <u>love</u> it that you send pictures with your letters !! I can't wait to see the sea life ones! I will have to take you up on your offer to take me sailing when I get out. I must say I prefer to go in nice weather though. Is that okay?*
>
> *Thank you for your kind words about the situation with my mom. It is hard to talk to <u>any</u> of the family members. Everyone gets so emotional.*
>
> *If you are considering coming to visit we will need to get you approved on my list. I don't have your information yet, but as soon as I do I will submit it. Do you think it will be awkward at all? I've never had a visit that wasn't a family member yet so I wouldn't know. I would not be ready for a kiss though so you would have to promise to be on your best behavior .*

Letters from Prison

> *The information I would need is you DOB, SS# <u>and</u> if ya have ever been in any trouble in the past. If I do not tell the truth on that part, I get in trouble, so please be honest.*
>
> *By the way - I always tell the truth. Sometimes I may choose not to answer a question, but I was raised not to lie.*
>
> *I must say I am glad to have you as a friend. I hope you are doing well. Don't work too hard .*
>
> *You are in my thoughts*
> *Always, Nicole*

Author's Note:

I wanted to meet with this women, but I wasn't ready to send her my social security number just yet... ☺

May 5, 2001
Dear Ed,

Thank you for another nice letter. I'm sorry if I offended you with the kiss comment. I didn't mean to. You did say that it was to be a pen-pal relationship. I was just trying to avoid feeling awkward in the visiting room itself, so I thought I would at least touch on it. I didn't know you were married and certainly didn't mean to assume anything. I hope you will accept my apology.

I enjoyed the story of the Humbolt State woman. Thank you for sharing it with me. It is encouraging that she is doing well .

You mentioned that you get satisfaction out of the small deed of writing to others like myself, however, I see it as a <u>very</u> kind thing to do. I feel very fortunate that you are here for me and that you take time out of your busy schedule for those of us with too much time on our hands!

Letters from Prison

I hope I am not getting cold after all these years. I guess since we met off the internet and I've had so many people deceive me in life, I just had to make sure. I hope you understand.

I would definitely like to hear the second reason and get your info for visiting. Are you still interested in coming?

Okay - now for the latest news. My aunt came to visit. It was an okay visit except that she brought bad news .

My grandma who just had her 75th birthday has advanced breast cancer (one of the worst cases the doctors have seen). She has known for 4 years and chose <u>not</u> to tell the family. Plus she's refused all treatments. I am told I will most likely lose her and my mom by the end of the year. Well, enough about this for now!

I've managed to get a cold this last week - Yuck! Hopefully it won't last long.

Not much else is really going on at this point. I am still in good spirits and I hope to hear from you again soon.

Much Respect, Nicole

Author's Note:

Given past experience with most of the prison inmates, I was waiting for the shoe to drop and the almost inevitable request for money. At this point, three of the five women with whom I'd corresponded had asked for funds, in one way or another.

May 19, 2001
Dear Ed,
    I love the picture of the sea lions at Crescent City. Thank you

Just like you I cannot stand to be treated poorly by various employees! I have literally <u>years</u> of CUSTOMER service experience. I won't go into it all here but I spent 3 years at Symantec. Before that I was employed at the Black Angus (Puente Hills Mall) in Los Angeles. I enjoy people and I always made great money interacting with them.

Your idea is wonderful for the Sports Bar and Grill. I've been wondering what exactly I was going to do when I get released (for employment). If my parole officer goes along with it I would really enjoy working in that type of enviornment. Plus, you will see that I am darn good at it.

Thank you for the kind words about my grandma. She is a very tough woman. She is full blooded German and I just love her to pieces.

May I ask you a question? (okay two - wink). You said in your letter that you told Deb that you wouldn't let her spend all you had saved without a guarantee of success and that you would work until you couldn't. Was this all hypothetical? I mean you and/or your wife are both healthy, right? You don't have to answer this. I am asking because <u>I care</u> and because of what is going on in my family.

Well enough of that! I am wondering if you will still want to come and visit sometime?

I am also wondering other things like how those bikers knew you in California, even though it is none of my business. I wonder if you used to be a little wild when you were younger and what if anything changed you.

I guess I just want to get to know you better.

I am happy to have you as my friend - I am glad you write to me. Thank you for being in my life Ed.

I look forward to hearing from you again.

     Sweet Dreams, Nicole

Letters from Prison

Author's Note:

    I continued to feel strongly that Nicole was just what I was looking for in an employee.

    Her reference to my wife's health and my own was due to my comment in the previous letter to her, responding to the news of her grandmother. I'd said that if either of us were to get inoperable cancer, neither of us would deplete all our savings, trying to combat it. I felt it would be somewhat selfish to use all you've saved to add maybe six months to a year to your life and leave your spouse with nothing after you die.

May 30, 2001
Dear Ed,

    Thank you for another nice letter! It really cheered me up. I've been a mess ever since my grandma died last Thursday. She was like my best friend. I could always tell her anything. I am going to miss her like crazy

    I am enclosing the visiting application for you to fill out. Then you can just send it back and I will submit it. My Mom is in a wheelchair and she was able to visit so they must have a wand (metal detector) that they use. You can call to make sure before you make the trip.

    The weather has been so nice. It makes it really hard to be here. I am so used to being around water. I am sure you can understand what I mean.

    Right now I am in an anger management class (well I am on break !!). It is a 5 week class.

    Anyway I hope all is well in Santa Barbara! I hope to hear from you again soon.

    Much respect, Nicole

Letters from Prison

Author's Note:

Each letter I receive strengthened my conviction Nicole would make a great addition to my team.

June 15, 2001
Dear Ed,

(laugh) Why yes, I do love animals. Thank you for the picture of Bear. He is gorgeous.

You were approved and placed on my visiting list. I enclosed the slip for proof. You shouldn't need it to visit me though.

I trust your trip to Fontana, CA went well .

My aunt comes to visit about every other week or so, schedule permitting. When she visits it is usually on Sunday night, just so you know.

I've enclosed a copy of the visiting hours/rules too. Sometimes I may be out running when you come to visit so I hope you don't mind a little sweat

Anyway it is late, but I wanted you to know all went well.

I am doing fairly well despite everything. I hope to hear from you soon.

Nicole

Author's Note:

In my next letter to Nicole, I explained the new situation with the IRS and the fact my plans for the bar and grill were on hold. We are still in contact and, in the event I can get the sports bar up and running, I hope Nicole will be a part of the employee team.

Pamela
Dade Correctional Institution
Florida City, FL

April 11, 2001
Hi Ed,

I just received your letter with your handsome face on it. You have a serious look that says I command the sea.

Your letter brighten my evening and you are right about the lack of responses due to my release date. What they don't realize is that date is being worked down as we speak. I get 10 days a month off my time for working.

I enjoy your picture and the reason is I can close my eyes and almost feel the wind blowing through my hair.

Yes, I can also picture you behind a 18-wheeler commanding the road. In other words you appear on a whole to be a take charge man. Since you teach sailing, does this mean that I can get free lessons? Smile.

Ed, let me tell you a little about myself. I will start by telling you why I am incarcerated. I know you did not ask but if you continue to write me you will find that I am very open and out front. In other words I like laying all my cards out on the table. I am incarcerated for Robbery of a department store. Yeah I could lay on the line about my x-boy friend but honestly the truth is I knew right from wrong. It was a foolish move on my part that has cost me my freedom.

> *Ed when I came to prison I was illiterate reading at a all time low of second grade. Yeah that bad. I use to be ashame but not anymore because I now have my GED, Okay so it's not a college degree but believe me I came a long way. I even complete a Business Computer System course. I've share this part of me with you to show that I'm shell we say ready to make a new life for myself.*
>
> *I am single, never been married, nor do I have any children. Family, none to speak of. I'm like the black sheep of the family so they turned their backs on me. And, yes it get's kind of lonely in here without people on the outside standing beside me. Lets see I am very caring but I can also be hard. In here some time you have to be hard.*
>
> *Have I run my new friend off yet? I hope not.*
>
> *I also am a loyal friend. In terms of activities other then sailing I enjoy a good game of handball and I work out daily to keep my body in tune. I read a great deal anything from mysterys to fictions. Anything I get my hands on I read. Could be I am making up for the years I couldn't read.*
>
> *Ed, they just called lights out. So let me close so I can get this letter off. If you are still interested I would love to here more about you.*
>
> > *Have A good Day*
> > *Pamela*

Author's Note:

Pamela's profile didn't really fit the criteria I'd established, but her love of sailing led me to contact her, when I assembled my list of potential candidates.

Letters from Prison

April 27, 2001
Hi Ed

    Friday night all dressed up in prison blues and no where to go. Hee hee.

    I received your letter this evening, and I must admit your picture is a very nice closure to my day. You are a very well built good looking man. The kind of look that says all man.

    That's really neat how through computers you are now able to post postage as well as put your picture on each letter.

    So you are a man of many trades I see. I'm sorry to see that your family did not turn the business over to you. But it may have been for the best if you are more happy on the road. Honestly from the looks of you in both pictures I can see you taking charge no matter where or what you do and in that case it is your families lost.

    I do know that family can often be the cause of much pain. My story is a night mare, but then I view it as somebody out there story is worst then mine. And if you hold on to the pain it will only serve to eat you up.

    Did I tell you I would like to start my own business once I get out. I'm thinking on the lines of a gift basket and personalize childrens books. I can start both with as little as $500.00 And since I will be starting from ground -0-, I look to get started after my first pay check once release.

    What I'll have to find out is the cost of permits ex……

    I have wrote classification and ask for a visiting form, they just change the way they process it so let me find out how it is done. I should here something back from my classification specialist this week and I'll let you know okay. I also may be going out to court soon. I am fighting to get my lost gain time back which would allow me to get release sooner. Anyway if there is any delay in our mail it will only be due to I am out to court and they won't allow me to take my stamps.

Letters from Prison

I had a court date for April 17th but Department of Correction failed to get me there, which could have been due to the court's failed to send a removal order.

Back to the visit if you send a phone number, which I am out to court I can call. That is if you feel comfortable with me having it. But then too you may be out on the road.

I'm glad to here that you like hips because no matter how much I try I can't loose them. They have always been big.

Ed, do you live alone or do you have a wife in every other city, hee - hee.

Are you driving down in the winter? Do you drive on your own or for a company?

When you're not sailing are driving what do you do with self?

My past time is reading in here anyway.

Do you like handball. It's a good work out for me. They don't allow it in here anymore.

Ed, tell me what are your days like. Remember you are my eyes and ears out in the free world. The unit I stay on doesn't have T.V. So I'm pretty much in the dark as far as what's going on in the world.

Well with that it's time to get this in the mail before mail pick up.

I look forward to your next letter

Pam

Author's Note:

Pamela seemed to be starved for things from the outside, more than the other girls who'd written. I suspected she'd been in prison longer than she implied in her website bio. If we continued to correspond, I planned to do a more thorough background check. At that point I was becoming more familiar with some of the finer points of inmate correspondence and expectations.

May 22, 2001
Hi Daniel,

Got your letter this evening and yes that is a really cool truck. Did you get a chance to take pictures of your new ford? What is a power stroke diesel? Now don't go laughing at my questions. I'm not that bad I do know how to change a tire here and there. Hee-hee.

So what did you do in Frisco? Do you have family there? Or just a friend are two (smile).

I'm sorry to here about that stories such as yours only reinforces my belief that I don't want to get married any time soon. On the road 311 Days is a lot of time, hell it sounds like you're more married to the road. You are laughing aren't you? If not I'm in big trouble. Hee-hee. You know Daniel that's very good of you to reach out to thoughs behind bars. That's good also that she maintain contack after she was release.

Yes in my case also your letters and the pictures of the out side cheer me up. I am currently housed on a close managment unit, which is where we are lock down 24 hours a day, We are only allowed to shower three times a week and go out side once a week for three hours. You next question is why I am on this wing. See I can read minds. Hee-hee. Anyway over a year ago I had a fight which I didn't start but I finish and the outcome for her was not good. Since the fight ended with me being more how should I put it more aggressive I ended up on close managment. I should be off by the end of the year. I have never been on these grounds other then C.M so I really don't know what it's like. I have heard from others it is all right. My point in telling all this is to say how your letters cheer me up.

> *Okay so what is your second reason for writing that you said you tell me about in my next letter.*
>
> *I really do appreciate your openess and honesty, it's such a good change. Lights out soon. I look forward to hearing from you. Pam*
>
> *P.S. Be sure to put my housing unit on letter*

Author's Note:

I noticed Pam used my first name, Daniel, on this letter, although she used "Ed" in the previous two. This led me to suspect she was getting numerous letters from other pen pals and was trying to keep us all straight. I was a little concerned about the reference to the fight and her being in lock down. Maybe that explained her heightened need for news of the outside world.

> *June 20, 2001*
>
> *Hi Ed,*
>
> *Got your letter this evening and I must admit I was surprised to here from you again. I believed with all the current information you would give me the boot. I was relieved that - that was not the case. Yeah I can see where the age factor could make a difference and it is true it is a young girls world. However this old girl doesn't feel old not by a long shot and I am not ready to give up yet. Before getting into a little more of my history (smile) since you are looking for young girls maybe I have some information that will help you out. From my understanding you got my name and & address from Jail Babe after paying a fee! Well, there are many other cites that has listing of prisoners along with there address, it is <u>free</u> to you, It's the inmate that pays to place the ad. This way you can check them out for free.*

Speaking of web cites what did you write to Jail Babes concerning me and my age? Did they pull my ad? Anyway here's a few web cites that I paid to be on. When you go there let me know if my ad is still running on the first two.

1.) Friends on both side www.friendsonbothsides.com
2.) Transcend The Wall http://www.transcendthewall.net/
3.) Inmate Classified webmaster@inmate.com or www.inmate.com
4.) Penpals-n-Prison.com http://www.penpals-n-prison.com
5.) American-Prison.co.UK
6.) www.cyberspace-inmates.com

Well here a few I hope that they help in some way to find ladies for employment.

Now to tell you a little more about me. When I came to prison I was illiterate sure I could read enough to get buy and count my money but that was it. I couldn't read most road signs or a newspaper. It was a wonder how I got by all thoughs years. Since my incarceration I've passed the G.E.D., I've also completed Office Technology and Business Computer Systems. I read everything I can get my hands on. Currently I am trying to find if there are any grants to pay for a Small Business Management Correspondence Course. If you know of any let me know. I do realize that it will be hard for me to find enployment and my age will play a factor but I am doing everything I can from within to increase my chances. I type 75wpm and will higher myself out aside from a 9 to 5. I also have plans of openning my own business once I save up my starting capitol. Yes, had I been younger I would have been perfect for the start up job.

Well Ed I've went on enough for now. I look forward to hearing from you.

Have a nice day, Pam

Letters from Prison

Author's Note:

Pam was right. I had contacted Jail Babes, given my building suspicions. Pamela had lied about her age and the picture she had used was twelve years old.

That nagging feeling I had about her being locked up for years was also correct. I did a background check and learned she had been locked up for more than ten years. Overall, there were so many inconsistencies in her bio, it almost constituted fraud.

I was also becoming more convinced she had numerous pen pals. The information she included in this letter regarding illiteracy and courses she'd taken was a repeat of earlier information she provided.

July 7, 2001

Dear Daniel,

First allow me to apologize for the age difference. If you are honest with yourself what woman do you know who hasn't put her age up or down. Okay maybe I am over stating the fact.

I guess what I am trying to say is all the information I have given you is truthful my charge etc....That pictures is of me, It's not a matter of how I looked clean up it's a matter of how I have been incarcerated since March of 1989 and the Department of Correction picture was taken this year.

I don't have a excuse other then my need for friendship was greater then the age issue. What I had hope was once you came to visit me I had a better chance at explaining. I was mistaken and again I apologize I only wanted to fill the lonely hours and contact with someone that doesn't lead a life of crime so I would have real friends.

I really don't know what to say beyong this point. Except could you get your Superior Court judge uncle to get me out. Just joking.

> *On a more serious note I ask that you take in concideration all the other information as you see is the truth and continue to be my friend.*
>
> *I hope to hear from you again I really enjoyed your letters and pictures.*
>
> *Pamela*

Author's Note:

This women was smooth to the end…

July 23, 2001
Hi Ed,

It was good to here from you again. Sorry for the delay but I ran out of stamps. That happens from time-to-time.

That's a nice bike, what kind did you order? I ask what kind like I would know the difference. Hee-hee. I may not know the different but I sure know how to park my butt on the back of one. Well.....

No I didn't know it rainned in Eugene nine months. WOW! That's a long time. Is it a lot of rain?

I'm really sorry to here about your troubles with I.R.S.. Damn you should have used me as your dependant. Okay, just kidding. Serously that's a lot of money going back to the government. I am also sorry to here about your club being put off. However you may want to use this time to look around for your employees. You seem to have had a bad week or to. I've never been married so I really don't know what to say on the subject. To be honest, I never wanted to be married. I really enjoy living alone. Does that

Letters from Prison

sound selfish? If so, I guess that is what I am. When it comes to waking up, I'd much perfer waking up alone. How do you like waking up in the morning?

Well let me fill you in on this end. Jail Babe pulled my ad.   . Oh well.

I filed a writ for past earned gain time sometime ago. Any way, I lost on the first level. This is gain time I earned while I was on a interstate compact That's where I was housed on the State of Maryland serving Florida's time. Well in between Florida & Maryland I was not given my gain time for working. Eight years worth. Yeah it's that serious with that gain time I would have been released like yesterday. I was kinda feeling down because the courts did not grant me this time, but the fight is not over I plan to file in the higher courts. So I guess it's been a bad time for both of us. The good thing is, it could be worst. So life goes on.

What I would ask of you, ACLU has a prisoner legal journal that I would like, it cost $2.00 I have enclosed a letter requesting it - it only needs the $2.00 money order.

Well that's about it for now I do hope to here from you soon and drive safe.

Pam

Author's Note:

I told Pamela that no money would be coming and the above was the last letter I received from her. I will admit she is a piece of work. I wish her the best of luck.

Christianne

Central California Women's Facility, State Prison

Chowchilla, CA

April 12, 2001
Dear Ed.
 Why, thank you for writing me. I'm flattered you find me attractive. - Nice picture of yourself. Wish I was on a boat right about now...Actually, I wish I could be anywhere else in the world, than here. - Oh. Well, my stupid ass knew better. I'll quit whinning!! - So, you find me interesting and I'm glad you had written that you only want to be a pen-pal- cuz-thats all I want too. I can be a much better friend, than anything else, I've always been scared of marriage, So that's why I'm single. I dated a jar head once, when I use to live in 29 Palms. I also love Harley's too. And I've driven a 18 wheeler across country my uncle use to have one - He died, But I remember, I had no choice to learn, He was drunk and I was scared he'd kill us. I kicked him out of the seat and I took over..When I'm in life threatening situations I don't think, I just react. Sort of like the day I got arrested - The story of my life, My mom says I don't think - she's right! I've been through Eugene a couple of times, My parents & family live in Portland, Oregon - and I've been there lots of times, passing Eugene. I love driving.. You'll have to excuse my letter writing, I'm in a hurry. I have to go do a work-out. Get all sweaty - that sort of thing - But, I normally write better letters.

I worked in the Education Office for awhile I hated being in there. I finally got out. I'm in Dental now - learning how to be a Dental Technician, - it's something I've never tried before - Most of the things here I've done. (out there) - The only other thing I had wanted was graphic Arts and it's a 2 year waiting list I'm told.

I was really pissed off when I received this time. I understood I had to do some time, but not this much.. I had a hard time dealing with it. But, I decided that it was stupid to be like that. I'm stuck, I had no other choice than to deal with it, and do everything I can to better myself and turn this into something positive, and its working for me. I was running too much, out there, its time-out now...

By the way I'm paroling to Oregon.. I was going to go to Oregon State to do my time I'd be under the "California Law" CDC, rules, I haven't decided yet..

As far as visiting me. If you still want after you receive this letter, I'll send you a visiting form.

Thank you for Writing Me, Christianne

P.S. My roommate, very good friend also wants very much to write you.

Author's Note:

Christianne passed me on to her cell mate Judy, and never wrote me again.

Judy
Central Calif Women's Facility, State Prison
Chowchilla, CA

April 12, 2001
Hello Ed:

Hope when you receive these few lines they find you in the best of health and high spirits.

Now I hope you don't get upset about me writing - but Christianne wrote to Jail Babes and ask to be taken off the internet - but guess they haven't done so. And she is my friend - and said we might like each other. Want to give it a chance??

Let me be the lady that I am and interduce myself - and we can go from there. I'm 5'2/130 lbs. - long brown hair and baby blue eyes.

I'm very single - white - and lonely. I'm very open-minded - have a big heart. I don't play games, especially with peoples feelings.

Like yourself - I love the outdoors. I don't know how to sail - but would like to learn. I do scuba dive - love the wind in my hair.

I would like to know all about Mr. Ed Whitchurch III - and I do mean everything.

I'm not shy - and I don't have nothing to hide - No question is to personal. So ask away...

> *I have your picture - And I have to say you are a handsome man. If you decide to write back, I'll send you one of myself.*
>
> *Want to take that chance? Promise you won't regret it.*
>
> *Take it Easy,*
> *Judy*

Author's Note:

Although I didn't contact Judy and had no information about her background or interests, I sent a response to her letter. It was obvious the woman was lonely and she seemed to emphasize that fact and her availability.

April 27, 2001
Ed:

Hey there...

You sure did bring a big smile to my face. And I do appricate you being so honest about the other women you write. Sometimes that can be a problem. Jealous females. Something that I'm not.

I always read between the lines that you have a good sense of humor. That's another plus.

Tough Trucker look - You look like a big teddy bear that gives great bear hugs. Do you like to cuddle? I miss that the most being locked behind these walls...

And I like pictures - So please do put one or two in each letter - that would be nice. Also enjoy is a picture of myself - the other girl is my friend. You don't have to send it back... The only time we get to take pictures is another X-mas, or if we get visits.

Letters from Prison

> *About visiting - Are you already approved: I'm going to still have to send you a visiting form. I would like to meet you face to face.*
>
> *I'm here for transporting/sales of drugs. I don't/didn't use them, just was into it for the $. Good $, but not enough for me to go back to it. Ever!! I've learned my lessen - and hard...I don't get out till Sept. 2004 - hope that doesn't scare you off. I paid this price - 3 times over.*
>
> *In here I'm learning a trade - I'm in voc. Uphostery - and have to admit I'm doing great. I'm proud of myself...*
>
> *So where do you travel in that big rig of your's?? I've always wanted to learn how to drive, but I always thought I was to short. (in height) Is it hard??*
>
> *As I can tell you like your middle name "Ed" better than Daniel. Is there a reason? My middle name is Rebecca and must people (family) call me "Becky". I like it better too!*
>
> *Alright - Gotta Go. You take care and hope to hear more from you.*
>
> *Always's Your friend, Becky*
>
> P.S. Ann said hello!

Author's Note:

I continued to sense a deep loneliness and had the impression Judy might be a good person, but not employee material. However, I continued to write, as a courtesy.

> *May 24, 2001*
> *Ed: Hey there...*
>
> *Check out those eyes - I like them. Stare at me!! (smile).*
>
> *Do you like being on the road? And what do you go by on the radio?*

Letters from Prison

Yes - you do have to fill out a different form (visiting) for each inmate. So enclosed is one for me. And once you get that note from the doc - I would love to meet you face to face. Do you already visit here?

What happened to your leg?? If you don't mind me asking? I hurt my finger at school/work today - I tried to put a stapler thru my finer. Ouch. It hurts - would you kiss it and make it all well?

So I have to assume you like baseball? My favorite team would be the Yankees. I always watch the serials. (sp)

Which of the internets did you get Anna's picture? We're just curious! And it wonderful that you take time out of your busy life to give us ladies a little hope for the future. Thank you!!

Is there anything you like to know about me? No question is to personal. Just ask! I promise to always be open-minded and honest with you.

It's getting so hot here - 102 today. And summers a month away. HOT...

Well Ed - You take care and drive safe.

Always

Judy -

Author's Note:

I think Judy's cell mate, Anna, was trying to get a read on which web site was getting the most play. I found her picture on four web sites. Anna was quite attractive and I wondered if she served as the draw and farmed the letter writing out to her cell mates. Judy wasn't unattractive, but she wasn't someone whose picture would have gotten my attention.

Letters from Prison

June 15, 2001
Hello Ed:

As always it's a great pleasure to hear from you. You bring sunshine into this dull place. And I do appricate it a lot. <u>Thank you!!</u>

Like that new toy - hararar - I want a ride - can I?? <u>Beautiful!!</u> *That's good that your friend gave you a loaner - but what is the one you want? You didn't say?*

Sorry about the form - I really thought I sent you one - but one is enclosed in this one. Promise!!

Trust and believe this I want nothing but your friendship - I will never use you or take average of <u>our</u> friendship. Ever!!

I appricate getting mail from you. I guess you don't get a bad feeling from me cause your still writing me. (big smile)

I do have a small favor - could you make me 10 scans of the picture that's enclosed. It's of my daughter Jene and myself. If you can't I'll understand - just please send this photo back - it's the only one I have.

Let me tell you more about me!! I'm the baby of 5 kids - 2 older sisters - 2 older brothers. - all live in Florida - and have never been away from home. My mother (rest her soul) died of cancer in 90 - and my father (rest his soul) died of a heart attack in 93. None of my family - not even my kids - I have three Jene 25 - Bruce 23 - Crystal 22 they just are to busy - I guess. I came out to Calif. (San Diego) in 79 and made it home. Worked hard at (25) a dancer till I ran across a bunch of crazy bikers and started running drugs - don't use - just liked the $ -wrong answer. No, this isn't my first hip up in this snake put but hopefully my last. I got 6 yrs. It 80% with two strikes - and have a out date of Sept. 2004. I do want to relocate once this is over.

> *I go to school - Voc Uphostery in here and I'm learning a trade that I can take to the street. I even like what I'm doing. (smile)*
>
> *I'm very open-minded - meaning no questions are to personal. So ask away!! Anything??*
>
> *O' you ask what my offense was - transporting and sales...*
>
> *I have a big heart and I'm sensitive toward a lot of things.*
>
> *Let me close here - You take extra care - and be careful out there on that open highway.*
>
> *Thinking about You*
> *-Judy-*
>
> *P.S. Let me know about the photo. <u>Thanks</u>*

Author's Note:

As you can see, Judy was again repeating previous things she'd told me, as though she's not sure what has been sent. This sent up a red flag, and tolds me I was probably right about the assembly line writing scam or she was playing several pen pals at the same time, which is not uncommon for inmates, particularly if there's funding to be found in the process. Nonetheless, I made copies of her pictures and returned them to her.

> *July 1, 2001*
> *Hey Ed:*
>
> *What's up? I was sitting here thinking about you - and knew you wouldn't mind me writing; so here I am (smile)*
>
> *If I was out - and we were together - what would we do on this Sunday Afternoon? Could we go out on the boat - a putt up the coastline or what??*

Letters from Prison

I'm going outside for a hour - that's all I can handle of this sun up here - it's HOT! Ouch!! But I want to go see my friends...

Back to school tomorrow - I did tell you - In a Voc Uphostery class - and I have got about 10 credits toward this class. I like this kind of work.. Before this class is over I should be ceritfied (sp). And I've heard there's good $ in Uphostery. Even at the boat docks - doing sails, etc. What do you think?? Myself - I'm looking for a good trade.

Did you get the visiting form this time? It shouldn't take much to get you approved - since you said you been thru it before...

Just got out your picture and was checking out your eyes - You have beautiful eyes. I do want to see more of them. Can I?

How's that beautiful "harley" running? You been out on it? Where do you ride too? Up the coast or where? Sure wish I was out - and feeling the cool/hot wind thru my hair. (smile)

Well Ed - I just want to shot you a few lines - So till next time - Take care - Ride free.

Always

-Judy-

Author's Note:

This letter had a feel of melancholy in it. I think Judy needed to talk to someone and she picked me to try and express her feelings. I knew this was an impromptu letter, because it came before I sent a reply to her last letter.

I'm no shrink, but I can only imagine the feeling of loss Judy must have, spending the best years of her life behind bars.

July 11, 2001
 Smile big!!
  Ed: Hello "My friend"...

  How's everything going? Myself in good health and great spirit. I really don't let no one get me down. I just smile - and that makes people wonder what I'm up too. (ha ha)

  Before I get into this letter. I have a small favor to ask you - and if you can do it - it would be highly appriciated ...We're haveing (sp) a "Photo Sale", that only happens once a year, and I would like to take mine. They cost $25 and the $ has to be on account by the second week of Aug. - we take them in Sept. and get them back in Oct. - I would really like this. Thanks!! Please let me know!! O.K. - that's out of the way - now to your letter.

  Thank's for doing my pictures - what do you think about myself and daughter? I'll be looking for them next letter.

  Now about your "club" idea - I think it would work - most of us ladies are honest, trustworthy, and loyal to the people we care about - So yes I think that's a great idea!! Can I have a job? (smile)

  Your truck is nice - double sleeper - walk-in? Pretty. Can I ride with you? (smile)

  O' Annie just tapped me on the showeder and told me to tell you hi - And I was telling her about your idea - And she said she used to mg. a resturant in Neb. - and she said we (her & I) would come up and open the place up. (smile) Trust we both know how to handle attitudes. (ha, ha) And we're always a lady....

  Now about your (our) visiting problem - I don't have no way to ask these people. Nada. But why don't we just play it by ear. Fill out the form - it takes 4 to 6 wks to go thru and I can't wait to see you.

Letters from Prison

> *I really like your style - and outlook on life. That's real important in a friendship. Don't you agree? Well I'm off to lay in the sun. You take care.*
>
> *Always, Friends are beautiful, Judy*
>
> P.S. *Let me know about "<u>photo sale</u>"*

Author's Note:

Ah, we're back to money. I'd hoped the odds were going to swing in favor of friendship, over the long haul. I guess, when Judy got the copies I made for her, she felt it was time to "POP" the question and check the lay of the land.

I found it... curious, I guess, that Anna always seemed to be right there, to make a comment or ask a questions. Granted, the two were cell mates, but Anna seemed to have a vested interest in Judy's correspondence with me.

> *July 26, 2001*
> *Ed:*
>
> *HELLO HONEY...*
>
> *How's everything going with you?? Sorry to hear about your troubles - If it's not one thing - it's another. But just have patience (sp) this too will pass. Don't you agree??*
>
> *I have to thank you for doing the copies of my picture. I do really appricate it a lot..*
>
> *<u>Thank you</u>!! And you did a <u>good</u> job.*
>
> *Did you get the letter telling about <u>us</u> taking photo's next month? I would really appricate the help - and this only happens once a year. So please let me know. Thank you!!*
>
> *I do understand about you still being married - it's cheaper that way at times. Right?*

> *And the fact that you have to put your plans on hold - doesn't mean it won't happen. If that's what you want - then it will happen. One day!! Just keep that faith...*
>
> *What about the visiting form? Have you filled it out yet? I would love to see you. (smile)*
>
> *I've had a hard day - You take care and I'll write again soon.*
>
> *Always*
> *Judy*
>
> *Thanks again for the copies!*

Author's Note:

In my next letter to Judy, I continued to ignore the issue of the photo sale and her request for money. This was the last letter I received from her. I was finding a relatively dependable pattern of dropped correspondence, when the money flow got shut off, or didn't start, in response to a request for funds.

Jessica
Northern California Women's Facility
Stockton, CA

April 14, 2001
Ed,

I got your letter yesterday! Thanks for the picture, looking Good! But what really attracted me to your letter was that you seem to have a lot of heart. Its very uncommon these days, ya know?

You said most of the women you write are going to be locked up for a while. Does that statement mean you are making an exception for me, or that you think I am going to be here for a while? (cause really, comparatively I'm not going to be here very long - 2 years is nothing compared to 10!) Well regardless, your letter did cheer me up a little, so you reached your goal. Oh ya I wanted to ask you what your sign was. Im a virgo.

You sure do have a lot of hobbies! Maybe when I get out and live a little I can get a few of my own, but I do like to fish. And I'm pretty crafty. I like to make jewrly, and stuff. I can pretty much make nothing into something. (of course that skill greatly improved being in prison, having to make do with nothing!)

An ex-marine, hu! Did you ever go to war? (J/K) Im sure your not that old. How old are you? Im 21. But Im not a "Baby" as all the women here call me, endearingly, of course. (Hey-Im legal   )

> *Well Ed, I hope we can become friends. I certainly need all the friends I can get! Would you like me to send you a visiting form? Please let me know, as you must be approved before you could stop by.*
>
> *Well I better go for now. I hope to hear from you soon!*
>
> *Sincerely, Jessica.*
>
> *P.S. Oh ya. Are you married? (just asking because you said you were just looking to be friends. It doesn't matter if you are Im just curious)*

Author's Note:

Jessica never wrote me again. I have no idea why, just never heard from her after this letter.

Jennifer R

Texas Dept. of Criminal Justice

Gatesville, TX

April 17 2001
Dear Ed,

How are you? You are my first response on JailBabes! I just put my ad on it about a week ago...I've also got one on Meet-an-inmate.com if you want to look it up too. I've had it up about 2 weeks. I'm still real unsure of myself about this whole penpal thing. Though I am used to surfing the net & doing the chat rooms . Thank you for the pics, they're GREAT! I love <u>boats!</u> Though I must confess, I don't know jack about sailing. I've previously been a power boat gal...ripping across the water at full throttle!

So, do you write many women? You mentioned that most of the women you write are going to be locked up a long time. I feel sorry for anyone that is locked up for any length of time. I'm only doing a 4 year sentence and I've got almost 16 mos. Behind me. I have to do 24 minimum. Hopefully, it's all I'll have to do. I'm a young, first time offender and I'm here behind a probation revoke. Which is easy to do (revoke I mean.) If you write other convicts, you probably know that.

So you found me only "maybe a little interesting"? Hmmm...Should I spice up my ad? You didn't really ask me anything about myself...I hope that doesn't mean you aren't interested, Ed? I'll go ahead & fill you in just in case though . As you know, I am 23 years old. I have long brown hair and blue-green eyes and a curvy cute figure. (I'm an ex exotic dancer & still have the athletic build & full curves.) That pic on Jailbabes is from 99 and the ones on meetaninmate are from 2000 just before my arrest. I haven't seen that one, so I don't know how they came out. Maybe you could send me a copy? I have many things that I enjoy doing, probably because I enjoy life so much in general. Some of my favorite things to do are shooting pool, water skiing, dancing, playing on my 'puter, cooking, reading, watching comedies, driving (boats   & cars), playing chess, SPOILING my 5-1/2 yr son, hiking, rocking to all types of music. I can go on & on!

I like to think that I'm a pretty complex woman & that I am also a great person to have around. I am honest to the point of being blunt & brutal, but, you can rest assured, I'll never lie or sugar coat it. My philosophy is: Don't ask unless you really want to know!

So tell me more about you. What kinds of things do you haul? Do you enjoy it? Are you married? (I thought I noticed a wedding ring   What were the marines like? What is you secret desire? Your favorite color? Music? Car? What did you dream last night? Best prank you ever pulled? Ideal woman? There that should keep you busy for the next letter . Feel free to drill me back. I'm going to close for now, I'll be waiting for your response. Be safe & take care.

Yours truly, Jennifer

Author's Note:

Jennifer seemed to be just the kind of person I was looking for as an employee. Her letter presented someone outgoing, with a good personality, and, I assumed, pretty intelligent. It sounded as if she tried to eat life up and I suspected whatever put her behind bars was likely a case of just over doing it.

May 08, 2001
Hi Ed,

How are you, cowboy ? You look like a country singer in your duds. I like it though . Yeah. You're about as married as they come. But I am glad you chose to be honest with me and told me. We're off to a good start. It's okay with me. I'm used to married men...remember, I'm an exotic dancer. Pretty much par-for-the-course in my life! You don't <u>have</u> to tell me <u>any</u> of the reasons for writing me or any incarcerated women. You are a grown man, Ed. But, I am pleased that you chose to share even one with me. I think that it was very noble of you to keep up with & take care of the girl that you mentioned. And I am always pleased when one of my "sisters" is doing well after release. It gives me hope & motivation of the future.

So just how many women do you write? I get the impression quite a few? Does wifey know or mind? You thought I'd be fun to write to, huh? Just because I'm bisexual? . That's cute. I guess then I should feel honored or what? . HaHa You're funny & sweet Ed. I'm glad you decided to write me to begin with. I sense that you are very interesting. Oh, by the way thank you for printing me up that copy of my other ad. I really appreciate it. Damn these pens! All my pens keep running out! I hate this that I am having to write in all of these different colors. Well, I'm anxious to hear what the "2nd reason" is for writing those of us that are incarcerated. And of course, my interest is peaked about this whole thing about not wanting to be vulnerable yet by telling me the third reason. I can't help but wonder, <u>what</u> exactly could you say that would make you vulnerable (to me) thousands of miles away - behind 14 foot razor wire?

> *Have you been sailing lately? I admit I've taken your pics out of you & the boats a few times. Fantasized about sailing away. Really, I do that with a lot of different photos. Even magazine photos. Escapism from my current environment*
>
> *I was curious where does the name "Whitchurch" originate from? I have always been interested in peoples heritage. Maybe because I know so little of my own? I'm also wondering, what do you see happening with our letters? I mean are you seeking something in return? Your letters so far have been pretty vague. What's up? Tell me something real about yourself, Something I can chew on, ya know? And by all means, if you have <u>any</u> questions to ask me, go for it. I think I've already warned you about don't ask unless you can handle the truth. I am pretty direct. And I have no reason to lie. The truth is so much more interesting! I always enjoy hearing peoples stories - nothing makes me uncomfortable. Feel free to tell me whatever. I'd like to hear it. Anyway, I'm intrigued & waiting to hear & share, so the ball is in you court! Write me soon okay?*
>
> *Yours truly, Jennifer*

Author's Note:

This letter further convinced me I was onto something. Jennifer was engaging, intelligent and, most of all, curious about why I was writing her. She didn't just assume I was writing because she was gorgeous. Jennifer seemed to instinctively realize I had a reason for writing, outside the normal realm.

Letters from Prison

May 20, 2001
Dear Ed,

Hi Sweetie! Great to hear from you again! And I LOVE the cute pic of the seal. Aww. So, tell me, how has the harbor in Crecent City saved your ass a couple times?

WOW! 16 inmates?! All women? Yeah. I'm not surprised about hearing that a couple tried to run a scam. I understand its pretty common. I'm nosey, sorry. But what did they try to do?

So what does wifey think about you writing all of us? Ha ha. Lucky, huh? Well, that remains to be seen, now doesn't it. Personally I think you're the lucky one out of us that we're writing. .

Hey! What makes you think I'm NOT a "Bond-ette"? . I could be you know! LOL I'm hot enough, aren't I?

Well! So what's the hold up on starting up your bar? That sounds great! Of course I am biased because I am very entrepreneurial minded . So in answer to your question, it sounds like a FABULOUS idea. Both generous (towards your employees) and beneficial to you - both because it's a desire & financially. I must say, I'm flattered that you would say that someday you hope to have me as your right hand man. I'd be less than honest if I didn't express my doubts though. #1 - we just started writing, #2 how do I know you don't tell that to the other 15 inmates? #3 What could you possibly have learned about me this quickly, to know I'd be "right hand-man" worthy?

I AM however, glad to "hear" that you seem to be a loyal person. That is a quality that I treasure in a person. I am also intrigued about the previous. I'm cautious even if I'm not shy about taking chances. Duh! I'm here aren't I?

Of course, I have at least learned to be more cautious now Making a lifetime of bad decisions will eventually (hopefully) teach one that .

Letters from Prison

A lap dance or two? Ha! If they were half as good as I am, you should've bought at <u>least</u> 10!   I guess, if I were to end up ever coming to Eugene. I at least could work in a titty bar if nothing else. LOL Not! Those days are behind me! Too bad though, they were fun while they lasted !

Yuck! Beer?! Gross! Myself, I am a chanpagne & mixed cocktails drinker.

I play pool - but I do <u>drive</u> the golf cart. A couple times I "caddied" topless for charity through my club. Does that count?

Viking, eh? Does that mean you're a conquerer? What's the proper call for a Viking maiden? I'm a Heinz 57 - Cherokee, Scottish, Welsh, & who knows what else.

Hey! Did I tell you that I have a 10 month old baby boy that was adopted? Well, Saturday he & his parents came to visit!   I haven't seen him since he was 2 days old! God, he is <u>so</u> BEAUTIFUL!!! WOW! I cried & cried & laughed & laughed! Definitely the most bittersweet moment of my life. (It was also the 1st time his parents & I met face-to-face.)   They're fabulous people, I adore them. Probably my best decision to date.

Well Ed, off this goes...I'll be awaiting your letter. Have a safe trip if you are hitting the road anytime soon, okay? Take care, Friend.

Yours truly, Jennifer

Author's Note:

Reading this letter, I felt more than ever Jennifer would be a great employee and a future manager. With the right training and positive surroundings, she could go far.

I was surprised she shared her visit with her child. It had to be tough to tell me these things.

Letters from Prison

June 6, 2001
Dearest Ed,

How are you, Buddy? Well I hope . As usual, I was glad to hear from you. That was quite a "puppy" you sent me a pic of. I love "Rottenweilers" . They're nothing but <u>babies.</u> I've never owned one myself, because I've always lived in an apartment since adulthood. I would love to own one though. (But then, I <u>love</u> <u>all</u> animals!!! I'm definitely an animal lover. As a matter of fact, I am currently embroiled in a "scandel" with rank here. There are a few cats that live on the unit. Strays that we feed. Well, one of them just had kittens about 2-3 months ago. We call her "Tiger". I'm one of the few she lets pick her up. Bares her belly to me & everything. She's my baby . Well, about a week ago, I was checking her over, (I do that), when I discovered a <u>hole</u> in her right rear thigh. A <u>hole.</u> I an see her <u>muscle</u> . So I immediately went to rank and insisted that she be caught & sent to the SPCA. I even offered to get her myself. One of our sergeants agreed to call the city, but he wont let me get her. And <u>none</u> of the officers can get close enough! So she's still suffering. I confronted this same Sgt. today and had a fit on him (he's cool & approachable, so it was okay). But he insists that he wont let me catch her because he doesn't want me scratched. But she wouldn't SCRATCH ME! So, I'm REAL PISSED off right now! Okay new issue:

Now what makes an entrance to a harbor too dangerous & small in a storm? I'm trying to recall the one or three storms I was caught in on my family's power boat - but I know that is incomparable.

Before I forget, I never heard the 3rd part of your 3 part reason to write us inmates did I? .

Okay, I've heard of shit like women pulling those scams like you described. Sending pics that weren't them. (When I came into system, during orientation they <u>briefly</u>

talked about it. They didn't say a whole lot - probably to keep us from getting ideas. But, they made it <u>CLEAR</u> that if they discovered any of us pulling that, we'd be charged with <u>Felony EXTORTION!</u>) Thanks, but no thanks! Besides, I'm sexy enough, that I don't have to lie . Hahahaha! Although, since you mentioned the Free info Act & I am pretty sure my "mug shot" is posted, I shudder to think what I look like. In my defense, I was 8 mos. pregnant, hot & miserable and had been sleepless for 2 days for diagnostics, etc. when it was taken. Not to mention, PISSED off I was in prison .

Have I told you what I'm locked up for? If I haven't it's no big deal for me to tell you. I am not ashamed of my crime & <u>yes</u> I'm guilty. I freely admit it. Even if I didn't tell you, you probably knew. My "victim" was my lover, & she was <u>only</u> 3 years younger than me.

Whoopty-do! Big deal! But I also didn't know how old she was until after the fact.

So, your wife's name is? And she's really <u>not</u> bothered by you writing me?

Your company idea sounds neater, the more you describe it. Now, when are you gonna get moving on it? It also sounds like a great opportunity for us gals.

I don't know if you realize it, but I could be out anytime between Jan. '02 & Jan '04. That release date is the <u>latest</u> I can be held. But I'm eligible for parole Jan. 12, '02. I max out Jan. 12 '04. I would like to hire a parole attorney. They have a <u>much</u> higher success rate. But I can't afford one. It'd be nice if I could get those guys that took care of me like I hear those other girls get. But I have yet to meet one of those. Of course, I don't ask for money. I feel real weird about that. I am a <u>fiercely</u> independent person. Not to say I wouldn't take it if a guy offered. I just couldn't ask . Ya know?

You're absolutely correct about me being tenacious. It is both a plus and a defect of my personality - at times. But I am also the type of person who prefers to be my own boss, which is why I've always <u>been</u> my own boss since I was 18. In Texas, topless dancers work when they want for <u>who</u> they want. We are "contract labor" so to speak. But we are also treated as queens by our clubs. Duh - we're their "product" too! And as a graphic designer & business owner, my only boss were my customers. (I had to work w/ my hubby & our partner. We all had to be in agreement - but I did <u>not</u> take orders.) Of course, that's not to even say I can't or don't take them obviously, I do. I just prefer & am more successful as a leader. Otherwise I get bored. And when I get bored, I misbehave.

Ick! Wild Turkey?! Crown Royal?! Beer!? Ick! (Champagne, Rum, Vodka, liqueurs, etc... those are what I drink.) Correction: <u>Used</u> to.

I don't know if I would've described the golf cart thing as a "riot". It was wicked & exciting, (for a good cause of course) though. And I made <u>BUCKS</u> that day. I think I went home with about $3K plus.

My aunt Deb has epilepsy, I've never heard of her having seizures too much though. But since being incarcerated, I've had <u>A LOT</u> of dealings with gals who had seizures. Medical care...well.... leaves something to be desired. So I've helped many women in the throes of seizures - usually just me and one or two other gals helping. It's sad how many people are afraid to help out in those situations.

It <u>was</u> tough to put Christian up for adoption. But I know I made the right choice. Does your wife have contact with her son?

Hey Ed, could you do me a favor? Could you "clip" my pics from my sites & duplicate them several to a page or something - maybe enlarge them too. Then print me several

> *copies? My friends around here keep bugging me for a pic, but I only have my originals of those. (Which I sure as hell am not going to give up!) It'd be a great & big favor you could help me with . (Winning smile), Okay, Pal, it's time for bed. As you can probably tell by handwriting, I'm at my limit . Zzzzzzzzz*
>
> *Thinking of You, Your Friend, Jen XOXO*

Author's Note:

    This was the last letter I received from Jennifer. Like several others, she suddenly seemed to drop out of sight and I felt I had no right to push or question the sudden cessation of letters. I still feel she would have been a good prospect for what I wanted to accomplish and hope she achieved success when she was released.

Sharon

State Prison

Chowchilla, CA

April 21, 2001
Dear Ed,
Your letter was a very nice one. It is nice to hear from people on the outside. I am very impressed with your boat even though I am scared of water. I want to return the honesty that you had in your letter. I don't really like to write back & forth with the men that write other women here. I have seen this cause many problems between inmates & I am trying to keep myself out of trouble. Please do understand if it were not for this fact I would like to have your friendship through the mail. No hard feelings I hope.
Always Krissy (my middle name)

Author's Note:

As you've probably realized, many of the women in prison used the pen pal approach and web sites to solicit money from the outside. I can only assume Sharon knew one of the other women I'd been writing and was told hands off. I respected her wishes and never pressed the issue. Hopefully, she served her time without incident and is living a normal life on the outside.

Veronica
Central Calif. Women's Facility, State Prison
Chowchilla, CA

April 21, 2001
Hello Ed,

And I hope that all is well when my letter reaches to you. And as for myself I guess I'm doing alright for a lady in my situation.

I received you letter yesterday and was very glad to hear from you. I must say, why is a very attractive guy like you looking for women on the Internet?. I'd bet if you put the same exact picture of yourself that you sent to me on the Internet you'd receive mail like you were a movie star. Try it, you might like it!

So you say you're not looking for a soul-mate, well neither am I. I'm just looking for somebody to keep me company during my stay here. But who knows what'll happen when I get out. And I get out before 10-19-02, I should get out either June or July 2002. And I'm looking for a good friend in my life. Will you be my friend?

I can see that both of us are lonely. My reason is because I don't have any family. What is yours? Honestly I don't believe your lonely because one, you are too dam attractive. Two, you have a lot going for yourself and it's just the life you choose. But its ok, we are only human. I probably could go on and on just by looking at you. But I'll save it for my next letter.

Letters from Prison

> *And in my next letter I'll send you a visiting form, they didn't have any in English. And I wanted my letter to get to you ASAP to my new friend. And Ed before I close my letter to you I'm just gonna be frank with you because that's the type of woman I am. Ed, would you please me a money order & stamps. I really could use them, like I said I have no family. And I really would appreciate it very much.*
>
> *And when you write me back please feel free to ask me anything. I'm flexible.*
>
> *Take Care, Veronica*
>
> *P.S. And thanks for writing to me. It made my day. Your photo is taped in my locker!!*

Author's Note:

    It appeared Veronica thought I was a lonely man she could exploit, based on my response to her website ad. At the same time, I sensed she wasn't quite sure and hoped for some clarification. I have to admit, I found her assumptions somewhat amusing.

> *May 11, 2001*
>
> *Dearest Ed,*
>
>   *I must say I was surprized to hear from you again. Why? It's because I asked you for money. Because most guys would say to themselves "who do she think she is? She doesn't even know me"! But you know what they say "a close mouth <u>never</u> gets fed. Anyways I was real glad to hear from you. And your friend couldn't of said it better that letters can be a salvation. And believe me it feels real good to hear your name called for mail. And yours come with photos that really make me curious.*

Letters from Prison

  Now I'd like to say that I hope that my letter finds you in the best of care. And as for myself, I guess I'm just hanging in there. I moved from another unit since the last time I've written to you. So please notice the change of my housing address so the mail will come directly to me. Thanks. Ed, I was looking at the photo you sent to me and I'm sort of naïve about boats. And watering holes. I've been on a boat once in my life and I was nine years old on a field trip. We went whale watching. I've been to see the Queen Mary, and in Louisiana just the shrimp boats. But my question to you is why they call that boat a Schooner? And whats its purpose? And are all those people waiting to ride or buy something off the boats. Or is that just a place where people go sailing? And what is a watering hole? Because for sure theres a whole lot of water there and I don't see any holes.

  And you see, I knew it? You just write these incarcerated women as a past time, and you probably enjoy it. Because I know you travel all over and meet many very interesting people. And can probably adapt to many life styles. And have ate food in every part of this country. And I also believe you like a variety of women. But thats OK because its all good! I don't even know you but I like your life style, its interesting. And I could tell by your letters you have a "Heart". Sometimes you could tell a person by the way they write. Some people tell by penmanship and some can feel it in the words. And I could be wrong about you but I'm hardly never is. Well let me tell you what I've been doing since I last written to you. Well they gave me a gate pass. This is a pass meaning your crime is not serious enough and you can be trusted outside these gates. Well I walk out these gates everyday to an almond field. Yes we pick almonds. But I'm the tool lady. I hand out any and everything that one could use out in these orchids. I just received my license (hope I spelled that right) for driving tractors today.

> *But other than programming I just relax and read books because its too hot to do anything else. And before I close I'd like to say thanks for writing me again. I enjoy your mail. Well now I'm going to hang out for one hour with my best friend England (she's from England) I call her the Blonde Bomb.*
>
> *Take Care, Veronica*

Author's Note:

Despite the fact Veronica asked me for money right off the bat, I found her both intriguing and naive. Come on, how many people don't know that a watering hole is a BAR!!

> *June 4, 2001*
> *Hello Ed,*
>
> *And I hope that all is well when my letter reaches to you. And as for myself I guess I'm doing alright for a lady in my situation. I decided to write you a few lines to say hello to you since I haven't heard from you. I know that you are a very busy man traveling all over the world and God knows what else there is. But I guess when you get time I'll hear from you.*
>
> *And also I'd like to say happy belated holiday to you. Well as for myself I just been so busy here. I try to stay busy so that I could keep my mind off of a lot of things, especially this place. I've been wanting to write you but I don't know if you have gave up on me or not. But I really would like to hear from you. Remember what I said. I'm lonely.*
>
> *Take Care*
Veronica

Letters from Prison

Author's Note:

>Veronica apparently enjoyed my letters, tales of travel and pictures. It sounded as though she was truly hungry for news of the outside world. It also sounded as if she was worried I might not write anymore and it was more than the money I might send that interested her. In fact, our letters had crossed in the mail, as I'd sent one several days before receiving this.

June 6, 2001
Hello Ed,

I received you letter yesterday post-marked 5/15, and I don't believe how long it took to get to me. You have to excuse my writting because I'm sitting on top of a washing machine doing laundry and I really want this mail to get out to you. Our mail only goes out Mon-Thur. I wrote you a letter a few day ago wondering why I haven't heard from you. They are holding our mail up due to investigation, hear. But they're catching up now.

Anyways I was glad to hear from you. Like always, your letters brings big smiles to my face   I'm sitting here looking at the Seals, did you take that picture? And have you ever touched one of those animals? That's neat! And I'm also looking at the picture of the Schooner. it's a romantic looking boat, made for just two people. Hmm have you ever did something on one of those boats? I bet you really have a fun sort of life. I like your style. And most of all you have a warm heart. I could just see it through your mail. Well now let me tell you what I've been doing. Well its real hot here and I'm gone 11 hours out of the day and by the time I get in I'm tired as hell working in an almond field. It seems like I hardly have time for myself. And when I do have free time I hang out with my friend England "The Blonde Bomb". She's my best friend here, we met in County and we go home around the same time. And she says to tell you hi and can

Letters from Prison

> *she get a ride back from you when they deport her to England. But I have to go now, clothes are done and people are waiting. And before I close you can send me a money order! It has to come from the <u>Post Office</u>, : it must have my name & number: Veronica ---#--- on the money order and just send it to the same address as you write to me at. I really would appreciate it, and it'll help me out. I'm really looking forward to it.*
>
> Take Care, Veronica

Author's Note:

Well, darn. I was crushed. It had been the money the whole time, after all. Still, I found Veronica's letters and comments amusing and continued to write to her.

June 17, 2001

Hello Ed,

    And I hope that all is well with you when my letter reaches to you. And as for myself I guess I'm doing alright. First I'd like to start off by saying thanks for the stationary. I received it last week but I never got around to writting you back. It just seems like theres not enough hours in a day. You see I leave for work at 5:30 am and don't come back here until 4:pm. Then I rush and take a shower because we have count at 4:30. And then theres chow at 5 and they don't let us back into our rooms until 6 to 6:30. And I be so tired by then I just get ready for work the next day. It even takes me longer to read books, I only read a couple of pages and I'm blowing Z's. And on Saturdays I play softball (3rd BASE), and yesterday we beat 31-1 just in the bottom of the 3rd inning. So you could just imagine how many times I ran around those bases. Plus its 101' out there.

Letters from Prison

On Sundays its my day to clean the room. I didn't go to breakfast so that I could sit down and write to my special friend - (U) But later, I'm going to hang out with England & Madonna and do the girl thing. And both ladies say to tell you hello. And yes of course we talk about you. I showed them your picture and they say you are very handsome. I say "I KNOW". Madonna wants to know if you have a friend to write her. She's gonna ask me what you said but I'm only mentioning it to you now. And before I close I need a BIG favor from you. <u>PLEASE</u> can you send me naked pictures off of your computer for me. No penetration, they could be of men & women. And one of you naked too! So I could see your great <u>BOD!</u>   We women would appreciate it very much, also enjoy it. In my next letter I'll be sending a letter from Madonna and maybe you have a friend for her. Please tell me in your next letter. Take care

Your Friend
Veronica

Author's Note:

    This was the first time I ever blushed reading a letter! (No, I didn't send her a picture of me naked!!) You have to admit, this woman was blunt and not afraid to ask for what she wants.

July 2, 2001
Hello Ed,

    I was just sitting here thinking about you, wondering where are you. I said to myself he must be at one of those watering holes. Or maybe delivering a schooner. Or maybe even having somebody fan you and feed you grapes. I just know I haven't heard from you since your last letter dated

Letters from Prison

May 15. So I just decided to drop you a few lines to let you know that I'm still living, and mostly to say hi. I was reading your letter and you mentioned about opening a bar of some sort for women. Have you ever seen the movie "Coyote Ugly". Its about some women who run a bar and make a fortune. So if you have or haven't you maybe could rent it and get some sort of ideas from it. But my personal opinion thats a cool ass bar and I would love to work in a place like that! Or even visit a place like that.

Anyways as for myself, I guess I'm doing fine. Still working hard everyday. Guess what I'm doing now? Alright you give up. Ok I'll tell you. I'm driving the tractors now. I never driven a stick before in my life. Now I drive vehicles with two & three separate gears. Ed your girl is doing it. Now all I have to learn is the fork lift to be certified and licensed. Mostly all we do on the fork lift is load and unload the hopper. (Thats the large container that holds the nuts) but I could get a job easily with that. Use some of this knowledge they're offering here and put it to use.

Also I'd like to wish you a happy 4th and please don't have too much fun. Well you take care and I hope to hear from you soon.

Your Friend
Veronica

Author's Note:

The truth is, Veronica's previous letter had left me reeling and I was taking time to decide whether or not to respond and, if so, *how* to respond.

Letters from Prison

July 15, 2001

Dearest Ed,

And I hope that all is well when my letter reaches to you. And as for myself I'm doing a little better since I've heard from you. At first I was worried because I thought you had given up on me. I don't know what I was thinking, because I know you have a very busy life. Boating, women etc, and big red truck!

Well as for myself I just been working hard on the farm like a Hebrew Slave. But at least I've accomplished a fork lift license. And I'm proud of myself. I could get me a job easily when I get out. I have to focus on positive things so I'll never make the mistake ever so I would come back here.

Ed, I see you are a man of many surprises and probably pleasures too! And I see you are gonna make my stay here very pleasurable. I think its exciting that we communicate through the mail the way we do. And we find out about each other little by little. And yes you could send me all types of pictures of all sorts of things. As long as you keep sending them on your letter papers. But no penetration. Even though I would prefer some. But I would love for you to send me some. And yes of your body too. I would send you one naked of me but unfortunately I can't. But maybe one day when I get out you could see it in 3D. Sometimes I wish I could tell you some of the things on my mind like my moods & feelings and even when I get "HORNY". But sometimes I'll feel I might be coming on too strong and don't wanna run you away. Because I'm digging your style; for you and as a person.

And before I close this letter you never mentioned again about the money I asked for. I gave you the information on how to send it to me. I really could use it.

Well you take care & write soon.

Yours, Veronica

Letters from Prison

Author's Note:

I did send Veronica some pictures I printed off the internet, ones I thought wouldn't get her in trouble. Since I had no desire to become part of prison lore, a picture of myself was not part of the package.

As you can see, Veronica was like many of the women with whom I corresponded. The bottom line was money, preferably sent on a regular basis.

July 30, 2001
Dear Ed,

And I hope that all is well when my letter reaches to you. And as for myself I'm doing better since I've heard from you. Did you know I'm grateful for your letters. You are the only one person who writes to me from my ad.

I was watching TV the other day and they were having a Earnest Hemmingway look alike contest. And they had it at a place called Sloppy Joe's, it was one of Hemmingways favorite watering holes. Thats the first time I've ever heard that word besides in your letter.

I see you've sent me a new picture to add to my collection. I must say you are a "MAN" of many surprizes. When you mentioned a 5th wheel I never thought of a camper. So is it fully equipped like in bathroom. And where do you travel to. And you probably take more than one woman at a time. I bet thats fun! I wish I could be a fly on the wall, or even a participater.

I'm really sorry to hear about you run in with the IRS. All I have to say about that is what kind of money do you make to be oweing that kind of money. Do tell! Inquiring minds anna know.

My room mate was just looking at your picture of your 5th Wheel and she says its really cool. So I showed her all the other ones you sent me. I told her I was waiting for the naked pictures. Especially the one of you.

Letters from Prison

  Also I think its real cool of you to be giving to charity. I was wondering why did you choose the Boys & Girls Club. Is there any specific reason. I know by your letters its not just a tax write off. I'm pretty sure your reasons are good.

  Your letter really made my day when you said I could get a rise out of you if I really worked on it. Are you saying that its hard for you to get a rise. If so you must be working with the wrong type of women. Because if it were me you'd probably never go down. You would have to go to a Dick Psychologist asking him why my dick doesn't go down. (I hope I made you laugh)

  Anyways let me tell you whats going on in my life. Well I'm still working very very hard. I'm also learning how to be a macanic. I'm just doing a whole lot of things on the farm.

  I don't know if you know about prison life, but theres a lot of homosexuality here. The problem I'm having is a woman is really chasing after me. She wants to do everything to me. But I tell her I'm not gay. Besides I know how to take care of myself when I feel horny. She tells me a woman could make a woman feel better than a man because she knows what a woman likes. But I know what I like and can satisfy myself. Believe me I do it all the time.

  And before I close I wish things turn out alright between the IRS & you. Because I really want you to open your club. And did you get any ideas from the movie Coyote Ugly. Who knows I might be one of the lucky women who get to work for you. Well you take care & write soon, and don't forget the naked pictures so I could have them when I take care of myself.

       Your Friend
       Veronica

Author's Note:

    In my response to this letter, I told Veronica I was a married man and, while my wife found her letters amusing, a naked picture of me was not likely. Veronica never wrote me again. I don't know if it was out of embarrassment (I kind of doubt it) or if she realized there was no more chance of her getting money than receiving a naked photo. I was somewhat disappointed Veronica didn't write anymore, as I found her spontaneous and amusing.

Deborah
Central California Women's Facility State Prison
Chowchilla, CA

April 22, 2001
Hello Ed,

How's life treating you at this time? Ed, I pray that this letter will find you in the very best of health and Gods Care.

As for myself I'm doing fine.

Ed, I received your letter a few day ago, sorry it took so long for me to respond. I had to borrow a stamp envelope. I normally don't borrow, because it leads to trouble and I truly don't want any trouble. I want to get out of this place. I will try and answer all your letters in a timely manner.

Thank you so much for the pictures along with the letter. And most of all Ed, thank you for being honest, about you writing other females here.

So you have a 18-Wheeler, you must be a very busy man going from state to state. I've never really treval, but I would love to. I came to Calif at a very young age, and I've been here every since. I live in southern Calif. San Fernando Valley. I have one sister, no children and both of my parents are deceased. I'm very lonely.

My sisters husband don't allow her to write me, for his own selfish reason. I love and miss my sister dearly.

I write her at times. I beg her to please send me money so I can buy the personal items a lady needs, but no response because of her husband. She is my sister and I know she loves me. True, I made a mistake, but that's no reason to take the only family I have away from me.

Ed, your letter really put a smile on my face, thank you so much.

Ed, I'm out of paper, I'll write more when I can. Please write again.

Take care & God Bless

Sincerely Deborah

Author's Note:

Yet another correspondent with no hesitation in immediately raising the issue of money and her need for funds. If you're keeping track, you've realized these women are, so far, in the majority.

May 10, 2001
Hello Ed

Sweetheart, hows life treating you at this time. Ed, I pray that these few lines will find you in the very best of health and Gods Care.

As for myself I'm doing okay.

Ed once again your letter along with picture of the sunset, put a smile on my face. Thanks so much for taking the time out to write. So you know what its like being the Black Sheep in the family. Ed I never had a large family, only one sister. We were very close. I don't know what happened since I been in here. She has a hateful husband.

> *Ed, the reason for me being here, I cashed my personal checks on a closed account. I didn't kill anyone dear. He shouldn't stop my only sister from corresponding with me. I love and miss my sister.*
>
> *Love, you mention about sending stamps, envelopes and paper. I can't receive paper in the mail. You can only send stamps or embossed envelopes. We have to buy the paper here. I'm unable to buy any. I have to borrow from the ladies here. I hate to because it can lead to problems and I don't want any problems. I want to get out of this place on my release date. I wrote my sister another letter begging her to please send me a postal money order so I can buy the personal items a lady needs. I still haven't heard from her. I cant borrow any more stamps & paper to write her, she wont write back. I don't know if she is allowed to read my letters. Its very sad dear, my heart aches I miss her so much.*
>
> *I'm sorry to hear about the relationship you have with your family. I cant understand it dear.*
>
> *Thanks for the beautiful picture.*
>
> *Sweetheart, I will close for now in hopes of hearing from you soon*
>
> *Take care*
>
> *Sincerely Deborah*

Author's Note:

While I'm sure Deborah meant to reassure me with the news that she'd not killed anyone, only written checks on a closed account, that fact immediately made her ineligible as a candidate for employment, particularly given the tone of her letters.

June 4, 2001
Hello Daniel

Love how's life treating you at this time? Daniel I pray that this letter will find you in the very best of health and God's care.

As for myself I'm doing okay.

Daniel, you've been on my mind all week. I haven't heard from you in a while. The last letter I got from you I believe it was the end of April. I've been looking forward to your letters and pictures. Please Dan was it something I said? Was my letter boring? Please write and tell me something Daniel, I would love to hear from you.

I know the mail system here is very slow. And I know you are Busy Working. Daniel please try and write me when you can. Your letter puts a smile on my face.

Daniel, love I will close for now in hopes of hearing from you.

Please take care of your self, stay strong and safe. God Bless you

Sincerely
Deborah

Author's Note:

Knowing Deborah couldn't even be considered as a candidate for my bar and restaurant enterprise, combined with the neediness she seemed to radiate and which I couldn't meet, I sent a brief note, explaining I'd no longer be able to write to her.

Lel Tisha
Leath Correctional Institutional
Greenwood, SC

April 22, 2001
Hello Ed,

How are you? Fine I hope . As for me Im okay. I was very suprised to recieve a letter from you. Your the only one to write to me. I guess Im important after all!!

It isn't easy being in prison. Especially when your family and friends forget all about you. I have 3 daughters and I can never see them again. Not a day goes by I don't think about them. I miss being home so much. So much I took for granted. So much I wish I still had. But its all gone. Im doing this time alone. And being alone is very hard on me. I never wanted for anything before. Now I hunger for it. I hunger for love, attention and freindship. Something I just gave up when the judge sentenced me. Someone I knew only 3 weeks took my freedom away. And thats sad.

Ed, I want you to know by you writing me it gives me some hope. That I am still human and someone took the time to write me. Your a true blessing to me!! Thanks so much.

Your photo on the boat is very nice. Im gonna always keep it. Its sad I can't put it in my photo album. It has to be instant prints and not computer pictures or

Letters from Prison

palaroid. We are not suppose to have paloroids mailed in period. But I do love to see pictures of the world. Makes me feel Ive been there. By the looks of your picture you love to sail. Ive never sailed before. Looks like fun.

Ed I promise to keep in touch as often as possible, but it's kinda hard on this girl cause I don't have the money to buy envelopes and paper. This envelope and paper I used to write you I hussled it. I cleaned one inmates shoes. So Im pretty much without. I never was like this before but as I said before family and friends forget all about you. One day I'll be blessed to have money again if its only a few dollars. It's better than none at all.

I've bored you enough. I do hope to recieve more mail from you. And if you want you can fill out the slip enclosed. Take care.

Just Me,
Lel-Tisha

Author's Note:

Lel-Tisha didn't waste much time getting to the point. The slip she referred to was a way to send her money. I don't know for sure if she polished someone's shoes to get the money to send me this letter, but it was a nice touch. At this point, I was becoming a bit cynical about the funding requests and some of the creative approaches used.

May 9, 2001

Hey Ed,

How are you? Fine I hope. As for me Im blessed to recieve yet another letter from you. Ive been looking for a letter from you this entire week. But I knew what a busy man you are. But still you found time to write me. I want to apologize for ever, ever sending you a money slip. Being in here is kinda hard without the help of friends and your family. But since I have No one I turned to you. Im very sorry for that. I use to have a job here in prison where I got paid $2.20 an hour. That was my way of survival in here. I lost that job because I flipped on another inmate when she said something that totally pissed me off. Don't bring my personal life up in the heat of an arguement you know. I was being pulled off of her in the middle of the arguement and I was accused of shoving an officer. Well I went to pick-up for it. I lost my job. My custody level changed. I got closed out. Thats like boot camp. But I held my head up high and I was determined Not to fall short to be listed as A sorry Ass. You know what Im saying. Well I was suppose to do 6 months but I only did 4 and I got my high level back which is an "I". Im so happy. So Im trying to get my job back but I have to wait six months before I can have it back. At least that's what Ive been told by the lady who's over all of the workers there.

  As for my crime I don't think I should hide it from you. I want to be completely honest with you, I was with A guy whom I only knew for 3 weeks that shot and killed someone. It was the guy I knew and his best friend. They pulled the gun on me and told me to drive the car. So I did cause I didn't want them to shot me. Anyway even though I told the truth about everything I was charged with Murder & Carjacking. The judge told me that the hand of one is the hand of all, because me being there I was as guilty as the person whom pulled the trigger. So here I sit with a sentence of 30 years for murder and 12 years for carjacking. I didn't even kill anyone. But my life has been taken from me and my 3 daughters. Tears fall on my pillow for my babies every night. I miss and love them deeply. I hardly get to see them. They are gonna be adopted and their father sells drugs and won't clear his act up to get them. You know with him *selling drugs he could at least send me money or at least write me. But he doesn't. Sad but true. Its like this is the deal I made so I shall lay in it for 42 years. But there is one thing I have excepted that's - Man gave me this time and Im holding my faith cause God didn't sentence the 42 years. And for God to bless me to have great health and to allow me this chance to have a special friend in my life. And I do thank God for you!! Ed your a blessing. From what you've told me in your letter you're a man with a Big Loving Heart. A Heart I want to learn and fondly respect for our friendship to always be strong.*

And to let you know Im serious about Not having paper and envelopes. Im making it known to you that I plan to be a faithful and honest person to you. Im very serious. And I do have certain inmates that are friends that will give me the paper and envelopes to keep in touch, but sometimes people will begin to get tired cause I know Ive grown tired of asking them. You see it in there eyes. And how they take forever to give you what you ask for. I can read between the lines!! Im telling you I will buy as many envelopes, pens and packs of paper to have to write you. You best Not get tired of me and pull away.

It's like I can go on and on talking with you on paper. And you know for you to be faithful in writing to many women God will truly bless you for that. I found myself smiling ear to ear when I get your letter. You brought a reason for me to go ask for mail. I been stop doing that but now that I have you I plan to check once a week. Ed I want you to take care okay. And if you want me to send you a visitor's form so if ever you stop by S.C. you can visit me. Okay. Would that be okay with you?

That was real sweet of you to help the lady out. Tell me are you an Angel? You seem to be to me. Such a sweethearted Man. Its hard in this world to find someone as caring and understanding as you.

> *And Im quite sure your friend is very very grateful to have you as the special person to always be there for her when you could. And I know I would feel even more the same way if the shoe were on the other foot. Its like a different world when your in prison. And it's real hard at times being in here. Hence sometimes ends up doing you And you find yourself alone and depressed.*
>
> *ED I pretty much believe Ive bored you long enough. I do hope to hear from you again. Im wondering will my time scare you away from me. I pray it doesn't.*
>
> *Take care. I'd love to see the new p.u. you got. I think the red one is pretty. But as always looks can only be looks. It's how it runs, sounds and feels. Be sweet until next time...*
>
> *I have a nick name I'd love to share it with you. But your gonna have to guess it for yourself. Here's a clue: Clue No. #1 - A nutt loner*
>
> *Always, Lel Tisha*
>
> *P.S. Im writing you anyway because I got the envelope & paper. But when I go to the canteen I'll buy the supplies and write you again, okay.*

Author's Note:

Lel Tisha painted a pretty bleak picture of her life outside prison, as well as her life inside.

Few of the women I wrote to were "lifers," as my original goal was finding potential employees for the sports bar. However, I'm human and possessed of the normal range of curiosity. In addition, after Michelle's experience, I wondered how many of these women were in prison as the result of bad choices in companions, particularly men. Lel Tisha wasn't a candidate for employment, but I was glad I'd contacted her, given the loneliness she was destined to accept and endure.

Letters from Prison

May 24, 2001
Hey Daniel,

How are you? Fine I hope. As for me Im okay. I recieved your letter. I haven't recieved a cooper reciept yet. I took the chance and decided to write you again. I love the seal. And let me make one thing clear, Im <u>not</u> working you for anything. Im real in all I do. I don't play games like that. And again I plan to be faithful in writing you. I don't get mail from No one. Im blessed to recieve your letters.

About my 42 years, well I went to court on the 15th of this month. I have to go back again in Aug. Im working on getting a time cut. Pray all goes well on that.

And the thing your planning on doing I hope it turns out in your favor. You're an awesome man to want to help people that are getting out of prison. You're a true blessing to so many people. And don't ever think about giving up your dreams. I feel in my heart they will come true. Im gonna pray on your destiny. And also let the other girls pray as well Okay. This isn't gonna be long. I want you to have this card. Hope it brings a smile to your face. I plan to write more to you on the weekend. Okay.

Clue #2 A <u>Bushy</u> <u>Tail</u>.

Always, Lel Tisha

Author's Note:

Once again, I was being assured my correspondent was "for real" and that she's not "working me," a reassurance I've already heard several times and have found, too often, to be a lie.

Letters from Prison

June 1, 2001
Hello Ed,

    How are you? Fine I hope. As for me Im so tired. I cut grass today and I got sun burnt pretty good today!! I have to cut more on tomorrow. I love the out doors. Its just when it get real hot I can't stand it.

    Yes I did go back on a P.C.R. in March. I have to go again in Aug. Im working on getting some of this time cut. God is with me on this.

    I thank you so much for being sincere about <u>writing</u> to me. That touched my heart. You are such A blessing to me, Not only to me but to other women also. Tell your wife she's blessed to have such a loving hearted man such as you.

    I feel you on the statement about people treating customers like shit. Ive been in the same boat. Even if Im the one being the person behind the counter And my customer is acting Nasty towards me, it's fine, cause I'll still be very considerate towards them. You know. Plenty of time you have to swallow that pride and do your job. To be for real about your idea - it's the Bomb!! Meaning I think its great. Go for it. I feel you'll be helping so many ex cons. And I feel in my heart they will feel very grateful and truly blessed. I got faith in you Ed. I think you can do it. And sure enough if I get out I plan to look you up for me a job. And As long As it's possible I plan to write you in return. Don't you go getting bored on me Now!! Okay.

    And the Night I decide to get a slip our officer station doesn't have any visitor's form. I haven't forgotten. I do plan to send you one. Okay?

    Have you yet to figure out my Nickname yet? If you need Another clue just let me Know okay.

Well Ed I just got in from the gym. I played 5 games of volleyball. And yes my team won most of them 4 games to 1. And that something. I can't wait for the coach to get A basket ball tournement going.

Do you have a favorite basketball team? I do. it's the "Lakers". My favorite players are Kobe Bryant and Shaq. They are untouchable. Kobe is my favorite. I got pictures of him all in my locker.

Well Im gonna end my letter Now. Hope to hear from you once again. Did you get your Father's Day card I sent you? Hope so. Hope you like it.

 Bye Ed

   Take care, Until later

    Lel Tisha

June 19, 2001

Hello Ed,

 How are you? Fine I hope. As for me Im okay. I was so happy to recieve 2 letters from you. Im glad you liked your Father's Day card. And do believe you are very welcome. The sunset in Seattle is very lovely. I was impressed also with the picture from Canada. It must be fun to go all over the world. Ive seen different things. But you know when I sit and look at the pictures you send me I feel as if Im traveling with you. As if Im seeing it myself. Thank you for that.

 I love that bike. Real Nice. I can just see you riding it. Just chilling!! Ive never rode a bike before. Maybe a bicycle!! That's as far as I've gone. One day I hope to ride a bike like you.

> I've recieved a visit from my family court lawyer. I was a bit surprised. She seems to be a lawyer that wants to really work hard for me. And I like that. Never before has a family court lawyer come to see me. Im trying to stop D.S.S. from taking my parental rights. Its so wrong. The God Mother that has the 2 older girls will not let me write to them or call them. The way I see this - she doesn't want us to love & bond. And I trusted her. But I guess I went wrong with her. Ive never been apart from my children, in so long of a time that we've been apart. Whenever _ever_ D.S.S. brings them to the prison to see me you can see the powerful bonds we share. I believe No one can ever take that away. You know? I can only leave this up to God.
>
> Did you have a wonderful Father's Day? Hope ya did!! This will be my 4th jail in prison soon. It's July 20th I'll be the big "29" !!!!
>
> Well Ed I think Ive bored you enough. Im gonna end my letter for now.
>
> Take Care
Write back soon.
Always Lel Tisha

Author's Note:

I often sent pictures of the places I'd been and I almost always got the same reaction. I can only imagine how much it meant to see far away places, when one was confined to a very small place with concrete and metal boundaries.

July 10, 2001
Hey Ed,

 How are you? Fine I hope. Hoping my letter finds you in great health. Happy your family is well and doing good.

 Sooo - did you have a great 4th of July? Just another day here in the prison for us. One thing was great - we had watermelon!! WOW!! I gave mine away. I wanted the BBQ Chicken instead.

 I've began to think you had forgot about me. But as always you surprised me. Thanks for the letter. You were thinking of me anyway. I did know in a way you were very busy.

 Again thanks for the pictures you send me. Im saving them all so that I can get a feel of seeing other parts of the world. Because I feel my soul needs to take a vacation other than this place. You feel me - I sit and just study your pictures and focus myself in different parts of the world. Relaxing and enjoying myself. You know. I remember when I use to take so much for granted, Now, I don't anymore. I see it all as A blessing.

 Well I'm suppose to hear something about my case concerning my children. It's suppose to be canceled. I have A New lawyer. She's pretty good. She's A blessing. Then I go back Next month on my P.C.R. I am so nervous about that.

 Yes Im getting old. But Im still looking good And so are you - Hey were Not getting old - we're getting better!! What do you think.

 That truck is so pretty. I just love parades. I just feel that those kids loved that so much. I can just imagine.

 Your still A good looking man with A loving heart, A sweet soul, and a very rare person to ever find in this world. Im very serious Ed.

> Guess what?!! I went to the Birthday Club Tonight and I had such fun. I didn't think I would have such A ball but I did. The clowns are so much fun. And the 2 church personals are sweet to.
>
> Hey have you figured out my nick-name yet? I know it couldn't have been that hard. Let me know what you've come up with I know you already got an idea. So let me know okay. And also I must say you have done A true thing for me. And that you have brought the outside to me. Thank you so much.
>
> Im keeping my head up. And also keeping my Nose clean.
>
> I'll chat some more later. I promise.
>> Take Care!!
>> Lel Tisha
>
> W/B Soon!!

August 2, 2001
Hey Ed,

> How are you? Fine I hope. As for me Im not so good. I recieved a visit from my daughters and at first it turned out good. But there was so much my daughters kept from me. See they are with their so called God-Mother. She has been treating my daughters like animals. She feeds them one meal a day. Im serious. She beat them with curtain rods, belts, thick sticks and telephone wires. Buys them clothes from A yard Sale. Sends them to school dirty and stinky. I have been crying since they came to see me. Theres so much more...But Im Not gonna bore you with all of that.

I wrote my lawyer about this situation. Im fighting for the father to get them. Im hoping God will come through for me.

Also I go back to court on my P.C.R. on Aug 15, 2001. Pray for me. My lawyer has ordered 2 of my wittnesses to be present at court for me. Theres A little hope for me.

My Birthday was A blissful one. Im that big "2-9"!! Im climbing that hill. I didn't recieve your gift. I didn't recieve much of anything. But I did recieve seeing A blessing to live to see my 29 years of life.

It's so hot over here. And when it storms it's so dangerous. At least it cools off for A while.

How's your family? Fine and blessed I hope. Well Ed you take it easy. Hope to hear from you soon.

Always, Lel T

Im only enclosing these cooper forms, I didn't know if you had some already. Okay. Might have thought that was the delay.

Bye

Author's Note:

The "Cooper form" Lel Tisha refers to is the form needed to send money to inmates. At this point, I'd not sent her any money for a while. Sooner or later, these letters almost always came back to requests for funds.

August 6, 2001
Hello Ed,

How are you? Fine I hope. Hope my letter finds you in great spirit and wonderful health. As for me Im Not doing to good. I mean as far as my health goes Im fine. Mentally Im Not. My heart is broken into so many pieces. Let me

Letters from Prison

begin by saying I had a visit with my 2 older daughters on last week Wed. All this time since they were with their God-Mother she has been abusing my girls. Their names are Britney and Jazzman. My oldest, Britney, told me so much I began to cry. But it's funny Not a tear fell. It all poured from the inside. They begged me Not to cry. To Not say anything to anyone. Not even D.S.S. But I have written to my lawyer. Im praying all works out. Im praying hard. Let me share a few things that my daughter told me. She said Mommy we don't eat but one meal a day. Thats supper. We don't eat breakfast or lunch. At one we eat hot dogs. MaMa we are forced to eat them. She showed me A bruise on her hand. Rather A deep cut that has healed, Anyway she said Mommy I was Mopping the kitchen floor, I put to much water on the floor and I was beaten by a curtain rod. The curtain rod went down on my hand. She said Mrs. Russell (The G.Mother) said if anyone askes you what happened to your hand you tell them that you fell off of your bike.

See the God-Mother is also A foster parent. And D.S.S. placed them there. I thought all along I could trust this woman. But my <u>judgement</u> was completely wrong, totally wrong. Why? Why? Im hurting so bad. Well their father is trying hard to get them now. Im going to court next Month on the 12th. Im hoping my lawyer can get the girls moved out of that house ASAP before something goes far worse than Now. Im so scared for my daughters. Im also going back on my P.C.R. on the 13th of this month. So much is going on.

Ed Im so sorry about your situation, but its all gonna work out.

Yes its hard in here. Very hard at times. But I do my best to get by. I feel like my entire world is falling apart. But I believe theres a God!! He's gonna see me through this. I know he will.

Letters from Prison

> *Ed you make me feel so special. Thank you!! I wish I had my own special photo of you, instead of the computer photos. A real one. One I can tape near me and look at and say I got A real friend out there. That special friend is you Ed. I pray we plant a good friendship that will grow into something strong and rich and so powerful.*
>
> *Before I close, don't worry about money - the one you were or are to send me for my Birthday. That day is long gone. So your having problems with the IRS. So its all good. Your letters are more important to me.*
>
> *Well Im "crashing". Take Care.*
>
>

Stay forever Sweet

Always Lel

>
> *P.S. Have you yet figured out my nick name yet?*

Author's Note:

    Either Lel Tisha was so upset about her children, she'd forgotten she'd already told me much of this or she was writing to more than one man and wasn't sure what she'd told each of them. I'll admit I was surprised she wasn't upset I hadn't sent any money.

    What Lel didn't know was that I'd done a background check and discovered the picture she'd sent me wasn't of her. This wasn't uncommon. Many of the inmates used a photo of an attractive friend or relative, as a way of attracting attention. It seems men are more tempted to offer letters and financial assistance to pretty ladies. While I appreciated her concern for her children, the fake photograph had me questioning the credibility of much she'd told me.

    In my next letter, I called her on the phony photo and some of the inconsistencies I'd found between her letters and her criminal record. I never heard from her again.

Gail
Central Calif. Women's Facility, State Prison
Chowchilla, CA

Ed,

    I recieved your letter tonight and am very pleased to meet you. I would be pleased to write you and become friends and I have time to establish that with you. I love the picture, and I love Harleys, I have my chaps and Jacket and boots still. I went on a few runs in Alaska and it was great. I'll take your attraction to me as a compliment, thank you, your quite handsome yourself.

    You mentioned writting other women, thank you for your honesty, I like that, hopefully I'll get special attention along the way! unfortunately I have no family out there to help me through this tuff time in my life so I have to be honest myself and ask if you can help me out so I can get some stationary and writting materials so I can continue writting to you. Thank you! I am really happy to recieve this letter. I've had a few letters but nothing interesting to me. You definitely got my interest, that's for sure.

    No, its not easy being locked up, sure you've heard it by your other pen-pals, but I only can speak for myself. I really get sick how these women disrespect there familys on the phones and don't appreciate them doing for them, its just not enough for them. What I'd give to have a family out there to be there for me, But I don't and all I can hope for is to be found by someone like yourself. I would appreciate *any help one can do to make this night mare a little easier. Writting materials and hygienes is all I need to be happy, I couldn't ask for no more. I want you to know this cause I see how these women can be and it makes me sick. I just had to say this from the start, and I'm sure you know we only can be sent money orders.*

You definitely put a smile on my face, and I hope I can do the same for you. I would love to visit with you when your in the area, I'll send you a form the next time I write. Let me take a guess, you ride a Heritage Harley! Am I wrong or right! Don't worry about me dropping out of your life, because I'm here just as you choose to be for me. Nice to know something about me excites you, I'm flattered.

I got your picture posted right next to my bed so I can look at you every day now. Please send me more pictures, I could enjoy brightening up my area with photos of you. I really miss fishing, bet you do alot of that too! The best fishing to me was in Alaska, its great. I see you got a good sence of humor, I like that. To be able to smile and laugh is very healthy. I stay as happy as possible with myself under my circumstances, but now I have something to smile and think about, "you"!

So until I hear from you again, know your thought of by me. Once I get some writting materials I will be writting quite often, around 3times or so a week. So I'm gonna go now. Thank you for coming into my life and caring enough to do so. Your gonna love being my friend, I promise you that.

Love, Gail

Author's Note:

    Send money. The common thread, although Gail didn't even wait to get acquainted. Nice touch, the subtle hint that the only way we could correspond was for me to finance her writing materials.

I'm a big hearted guy and this was early in my prison pen pal career, so I gave Gail the benefit of the doubt and kept writing her.

May 4, 2001
Ed III   ,

I just recieved your letter dated April 30th, what a nice letter. I was very happy to hear from you. I have to say this first and that's is that I understand why you feel the way you do about sending money to women because everyday I see how unappreciative these <u>bitches</u> (excuse my French) can be to have family and people helping them feel comfortable in a bad situation and it's just not enough and that makes me sick. Sure to have hygienes or a soda or a bag of chips, it would be nice but <u>me</u>, I never had anyone do anything to make it possible to even buy a nice bar of soap or good toothpaste, that would be heaven to me, but what ever you do for me I want to know it came from your heart and knowing that I would appreciate it and as far as sending some stationary that would be wonderful so I can write when ever and I wouldn't have to wash someones dirty clothes to get a few stamped envelopes, but believe me I will and have so I can write you. I just want to write when ever I choose. Thank you for sharing your 1 of 3 rules of thumb to me, and when you feel I've earned your trust and become close you can share anything with me, I charish and give you my honest opinion too, thats what friends are for and we have plenty of time to establish a friendship. Any women would be a fool to give another your address to write you, unless of course you wanted her to give out your address to other women, me myself, please don't ask cause I don't want to do that, I want you to do that on you own, I'm happy your writting me and I want it to stay that way. As far as you writting other women, thats your choice and I think its nice you put a smile on peoples faces. You writting me is a blessing and I'll charish each one you write. You say you write lifers and others you get a certain feeling from, so may I ask, what is it you felt for me to make you write me? Of course I still want you to write, don't be so silly. I will not ask you for nothing, and I mean that, just know if you ever surprize me with presents I'll appreciate it with all my heart. You said you understand the needs of a women in my place and how you understand, just know it's by my friendship or love, I just had to let you know how I feel. You're a very kind man and thats the Bomb!

Good definately comes to good and you picked a winner this time (ME)   You would look good in a heritage, thats a beautiful Bike. I'm sure one day you'll have one. So when is your birthday? do you have family? tell me your favorite foods & color. What do you do in your spare time? do you like a cold beer or a table dance?

I'm really a understanding person and very open minded and full of spunk. I love a good laugh too. Well, honey I'm gonna go to bed now, so until the next know your thought of by me.

Love, Gail

Author's Note:

Gail was an exotic dancer, as you may have figured out, with her reference to a "table dance." Often, these women found themselves running with the wrong crowd and, eventually, ended up in the drug culture or some form of prostitution.

I wasn't sure, at that point, what Gail had done to land in prison, but I believed it was something along those lines. While I hadn't yet formed an opinion, I wasn't willing to rule her out as a future employee.

May 17, 2001
Hi Big Guy,

As you see I got this pretty paper you sent. It's beautiful, thank you so much, also thank you for the stamps too, now I don't have to borrow or wash for any, at least not for a while. So you been out to sea since the last time I heard from you or on the road? 411 Ha Ha! So do you spend much time at home? don't sounds as if you do. What do you do in your spare time? So when you work driving a truck do you travel out of your state to others? So tell me, how's your sex life. sure hope it's okay for me to ask and if it's too personal let me know please. Just playing though!

So tell me a few things more, What's your favorite color and foods? What is your choice of drink? I would love a cold Budweiser right now. I'm a sociable drinker and I love Rib eye steak, med. Rare and prime rib too. I miss them things, it's the little things in life I miss. I love to go fishing that's my peace of mind and I miss it so much. I also miss going to the Beach at night taking my walks.

I enjoy playing chess, and swiming, lots of things, but I bet when I get out I will never go to jail again, never. So tell me, out of all the women you've written, have you ever been a part of there lives out there too? You see, when I get out I want to be a true friend and be apart of your life till the wheels fall off. Well, I'm anxious to hear from you again.

It really feels good to get a letter from you, it brightens my days and I thank you for that. So let me leave you with this thought: "kindness is more important than wisdom, and the recognition of this is the beginning of wisdom."

Take Care My Friend,

Love, Gail

Letters from Prison

Author's Note:

Gail seemed to be real, but I'd already learned the reason many of these women put their names and addresses on the internet was to solicit money from the outside. My gut told me Gail was no exception, but only time would tell.

May 21, 2001
Ed,

    Hi honey! Once again you put a smile on my face by recieving a letter from you. The picture of the seal is cute, yes I like it very much. Yes, I recieved the writting materials, thank you so much. As far as sending me some funds, you write it out to me to the same address except the P.O. Box number is different, it's 94 for money sent and it has to be sent in an envelope by it's self, can't have no letter in it or they'll send it back, so once again funds sent in my name to P.O. Box 94 and letters to P.O. Box 92. Thank you for the thought, it would be nice to have some hygienes.

    You told me how you see me when you look at my photo, your right about being social, but on <u>my terms</u>, but being angry inside because of my present situation, that is not correct, you see I have a spirit that's "happy go camper kind of girl". and I refuse to let being confined take that from me, and I stay happy with myself always. I'm kind to everyone, but being in prison you only can be so kind, like "hi and goodbye" and leave it at that. Also your right about when I do trust one, I will bend over backwards for them till the wheels fall off. Always take your time to allow yourself to use the word <u>friend,</u> that's to be earned, your very intelligent. As far as being there for me, I also will be there for you too and more so when I get out. About that club your considering, I'd make a hell of a manager! Customer service, I can definately handle, it takes a woman like myself to bring in the customers, and being the woman I am I know how to handle a patt on the ass, trust that! but in a very selectual way, with class & feness.

> *I enjoy beer, I drink <u>SOL</u>, its an excellent beer. You drink Corona then you'd love <u>SOL</u>, try it for me. I'll give you a table dance! there's nothing wrong with that. I myself would like to go with you to a titty bar! that's if its okay with you! You'd have a blast with me.*
>
> *I just missed your birthday, happy belated birthday honey, I won't forget you on the next one.*
>
> *So what area are you considering to have this business. Honey I just got called so I got to go now. Will write again tomorrow.*
>
> Take Care!!
> Love, Gail
>
> *P.S. I want a shot of Tequila and a table dance...*

Author's Note:

I found myself liking this woman's sense of humor. However, the idea of her as manager of my planned club was an altogether different story.

Gail seemed like she could be a lot of fun, but I felt she could also be a shark and a potential nightmare. She had the right attitude and might fit well into what I was trying to do, but I continued to sense it was better to steer clear of this one or at least go very slowly.

> June 4, 2001
>
> Ed,
>
> *Hi big guy! first let me apologize for not writting lately. I have a flu and it has me off my feet and very sick. I'm in bed still but sitting up writting since I'm feel a little better to sit up. I'm looking forward to hearing from you soon, I really enjoy your letters and I could use a smile on my face about now.   So how have you been doing? Been*

out to sea lately? How's trucking going? What is your CB name? I was just looking at that picture of the seal, its so cute.

Did I tell you that I'm in a new class/trade? I'm in Mill/Cabinets and next monday I go back to class and get to start my first project on the floor where all the electric tools and saws are and all the beautiful different kinds of wood. I'm really looking forward to that. I'll let you know when I write you monday after class and let you know all about it, okay! So anything exciting happen since I last heard from you? It's been beautiful here, up in the 100's, I have a nice tan. I just miss the tanning salons and getting the whole body nice and tan. Also when I do that I'm pampering myself, I'll do it when I get out. Honey, my head is pounding so I'm gonna lay my head down right now. I'll write again this weekend. Take care my friend and know your thought of by me always.

Love, Gail

Author's Note:

    It was pretty clear Gail wasn't feeling well, when she wrote this note. Not only was it short, by her standards, but there was almost a softness in her tone. I began to rethink my original impression of her.

June 7, 2001

    Hi big guy! Once again I have to pick up this pen and write to you. You are on my mind quite often. Looking forward to hearing from you soon. I know your a very busy man, but I really look forward to recieving mail from you. It brightens my day to hear from you. I love when you send me pictures that brighten my bed area up, being able to look at your face when I open and before I close my eyes each day.

Hopefully I'll hear from you soon, real soon! Tell me about your adventures while on water and the road. I bet you meet a lot of people traveling. Share some of your experiences with me, I can use a good laugh periodicly!

Anyway mail will be coming in the next 15 minutes. If I hear from you I'll write another letter tonight, If not I'll write this week-end again.

So gonna cut this off for now. Just know your thought of alot by me. Take Care and be safe while traveling.

Love, Gail

Author's Note:

Again, Gail seemed softer than earlier, as if she no longer felt the need to be tough in her letters and seemed to sincerely appreciate the letters and photos I sent her. Still, there remained this little voice in the back of my head, telling me to watch out. Perhaps I'd become more cynical, given my other experiences to date.

June 12, 2001

Daniel,

hi big guy! I recieved your letter and I'm sorry I didn't get back the same day I recieved it, but I got really sick and I had to go to the infirmary and come to find out I got food poisoning from the food here, I'm sore from being so sick, but I'm okay now. I'm scared to eat. I need to get my own food so it would be nice if you can help me so I can buy some groceries, please! A nice bike you got, it looks really nice. It fits you though. You are funny, and being kinky is just fine with me, it sounded good to me. I'm saying in reply to your letter that the bike you got is nice, and the kinky side of you, that's cool.

Letters from Prison

> *I like VO and seven too also Crown royal with a squirt of Cola is nice too. As far as my social side, that depends if I like a man, I'm really a fun person, but lets keep it real, I'm no prositute, so the terms for you will be strickly pleasure. I may be a stripper, but I have alot of class and respect for my self, its good money, but I'm strickly business. No one touches me and no dates. Like I said if I like you than that's great other then that its <u>NO</u>! I am definitely a people person, people are attracted to me and that is good for any business, I'm very business orientated and I know what it takes to run a straight business keeping it nice & clean. You thought about me while drinking a Corona, that's nice to be thought of. Thank you I'm flattered. Try SOL you'll like it, I believe so. And a table dance for you can be arranged in <u>private</u> though   Limo service too sounds great for your reasons. Well honey, I got to lay down I'm feeling bad still, just had to write a reply to your letter and let you know what happened to me and that I need your assistance or I'll be skin and bones before long. Have to send money order in an envelope by its self, no letter in it and mailed to same address except the Post Box is 94, the 92 Post Box is for letters only. Thanks Ed, if it's a problem don't worry, I still like you the same, I promise.*
>
> Love, Gail

Author's Note:

I had a little trouble believing she got food poisoning and the rest of the women were apparently fine. It was a new approach, however – "The food here made me sick, so send me money!" Apparently, that little voice of caution was right. Nonetheless, I did send her a small amount of money. Call it a reward for creativity.

More to the point, in terms of my plans, it appeared Gail was strongly considering going back to work as a stripper. I got the impression her stay at Camp Chowchilla was just a stopover, until she could get back to business.

June 15, 2001
Ed,

    hi big guy! I recieved your letter and the funds, thank you so much, I appreciate it very much. Every time I hear from you, you put a smile on my face and I laugh. You're a nut and I love it. I like the picture you sent of you 10 years ago. You go you big Stud! I wish you where here too and not being nice either! He He

    Sure hope your not working too hard, all work and no playing is not good for you. Go out and get you a table dance and a shot of tequila then let me know how it was.
So your going camping on the 4th of July with your grandparents how fun. I love camping and fishing and stuff. You have a nice time, think about me when you look up at the sky at night and see that one bright star, that's me winking at you.

    Yes, I'm working with many electrical saws, I'm very careful. I use the proper safety items always, push stick so my hands are not close to the blades. I just finished building 3 Book Cases with front double doors and reversible shelves and wall mounted, out of Oak, there beautiful. I really enjoy this trade. In about 5 months I'll graduate and have all my Certificates, I have 3 already. I'm gonna also get my universal EPA license for Optical Eye Wear and refrigeration and air conditional and if I have enough time to do one more trade it will be welding. I have to do positive things and take full advantage of these trades available to me while I'm here. How funny the story about the girl drunk off her ass. You say we look alike and that I'm better built, thank you for the complement, thats mighty nice of you. flattery will get you every where with me, ALMOST! Ha Ha

Letters from Prison

> *The truckers are really that stupid and immature on them CB's! I would think at times you can get a female on the line and talk a bit. Now are the women at the truck stops like they say? hot to trot? Your so funny Ed, you have a great sense of humor, I like that. It's very health minded to be able to laugh. I want you to know I really love your letters, you make my day every time I recieve a letter from you. Well my friend I got to jump in this shower and let the water hit between these thighs. Know your always thought of by me.*
>
> Love, Gail

Author's Note:

I have no idea why I continued writing to this woman, knowing full well she wasn't an employee candidate. Maybe my letters made her happy, and not the twenty-five dollar check I sent on occasion. Yeah, right.

July 12, 2001
Ed,

hi Big guy! how have you been? for myself, so-so! Sure hope to hear from you soon. I really look forward to your letters. I had to go have my eyes checked and there sending me to an eye-doctor to see if I have to wear glasses, yuck! anyway, tell me what you did on the 4th of July! Bet you had alot of fun! I miss being free, but I thank God I'm gonna get out cause a lot of women in here will never go home and so many young people, 18 years and up.

It's really sad, but I'm just thankful I will get out. We are definately gonna have to go out and have fun. So you been out in the water since the last letter you wrote me? I just ran out of ink so I'm using a colored pencil so excuse the writting. I'm in a new room, everythings the same on the letter address except you use V.S.P.W.#######, this is a nice room too. I changed to a regular pencil, oh well! My job was closed today, I'm setting here all by myself and it's so quiet, I love it. Think I'll hit the shower and let the water do its duty between these thighs! Yes, I said it and I ment it too. I sure hope I hear from you soon, I look forward to getting mail from you. Ed since I was real sick from the food, I've been loosing weight cause I can't eat the food here, I been eating fruit and peanut butter and jelly. Can you help me get a few groceries each month, not much but about 25. - a month? I'd appreciate it.

I'm gonna hit the shower big guy, and I write again soon. Drive safe, always.

Love, Gail

Author's Note:

Peanut butter and jelly, along with some fruit, was all she was eating? And it was suddenly my responsibility to buy her monthly groceries, even though she asked nicely? Even a big, dumb trucker like me had to see through this one. Nope, not bighearted Ed.

July 14, 2001
Ed,

Received your letter tonight and was happy to hear from you. I sent you a letter out today, that was before mail came. So I'll mail this in the morning on my way to work. You sure made me laugh from reading your letter. You never seem to amaze me. Nice picture of the truck, this is the truck you drive? Sounds like you had to bite your tongue while daddy was given you orders! It's still nice of you to spend the time you did with your family. Wish I had a family. Be good to yours your blessed to have one. I believe if mine kept me instead of giving me away as a baby, I truly believe I would of choosen a better road to go down.

This is a very touchy situation for me because I honestly can't answer any questions when asked about my family and it really hurts not knowing. Please try to understand that if I could say more I would, but I can't and that bothers the hell out of me. So lets move on further in your letter, okay!

It's nice your fathers wife is nice to you, that makes it nice. You did say that this truck was one your driving, looks very nice and comfortable. So you drive others? or just this one? I'm not trying to tease you, being nose to nose or ever nose to where ever else, that sounds real good, so are you trying to tease me? Sucks that I.R.S. is messing with you. I hope everything works out for you. You're a good man and you'll be blessed for the goodness you give to others. I'm no saint but I honestly believe it goes like that. Your goals to have your own business will happen if its ment to be. Did you get that good lay you said you needed after getting IRS on your ass? Wish I could help you out but your on you own till I can help you out in that department. I'll take a rain check! I want details on the table dance. Yes, take notes! Ha Ha I could use a table dance and a shot of tequilla myself! It's really nice to know that no matter what, you know I'm here and it's real shitty.

The letters are wonderful from you and I thank you for picking me to be a friend. It will always be straight forward. Sure this place sucks. Bitches in here make me sick. Only thing is of greed from these bitches. Yah, I wish I could shop once a month so I can shower with a nice bar soap and shampoo & conditioner, or eat a Candy bar and more, but I refuse to stress myself because I don't have no one out there to help me out. Yes, I have you and Yes I *would love to shop 25. - or even more so I can treat my body like I'm use to, smelling good and be able to eat something and know I'm not being poisoned by being fed old food. I'm not gonna make excuses's or lie to you just to get a few bucks so I can have these needs, I'm just being real and letting you know exactly how it is. I want to be loved for me and someone to care enough to understand! I really appreciate the time you take to write me and allowing me this time to establish a friendship with you and will continue even when I get out, but while I'm here I really need a friend and care enough to understand and help me. Well, Ed it's late and I have to get up in a few hours so let me close for now. I'll write again soon.*

Take Care Big Guy and don't forget to take notes.

Love, Gail

Author's Note:

I hadn't sent Gail a check for over a month and she was quietly complaining about the lack of funds between the lines. At this point, I'd learned to recognize the pattern and I admit I was curious to see how long the correspondence would continue, once the gravy train was shut down.

August 9, 2001
Ed,

hi big guy! I'm sure missing hearing from you. Sure hope your okay. Maybe too many table dances and shots of tequila? Ha Ha So tell me what you've been doing. This letter is gonna be short because I worked my butt off today and I'm drained and ready to go to bed, my bed is calling me! I don't know if I told you but at the end of this month I'll be gone a week, I'm a perfect match to save someone's

> *life, I'm a donor for a bone marrow transfusion. I'm nervous but I could not live with myself if I didn't do it and she died, so if you don't hear from me for a week or so know I'm gone but I'll be back, so continue to write. I'll write when I get back. So tell me, what do you do in your spare time and not working? I apologize but I have to close my eyes. I'll write again soon. Take Care and Be Safe.*
>
> Love, Gail

Author's Note:

This was the last letter I received from Gail. I have no idea how she was selected as a bone marrow donor. My last letter to her again contained no money and I can only assume it was the funds that kept her writing as long as she did.

Paula
Dade correctional Institution
Florida City, FL

April 24, 2001
Dear Ed,
Greetings and Salutations! I do hope this message has journeyed safely to you and found you in the very best of health and highest of spirits. I myself am faring well, despite the present locale.

I am currently in receipt of your recent letter of intro to me and its my pleasure to make your acquaintance. Thank you for enclosing the photos. Very nice vessel. I can see myself sailing round the globe on such a magnificent craft.

You were correct, unfortunately, in you presumption that it does get exceedingly boring and lonely in here. I spend the majority of my time these days listening to soft jazz and reading. I have a voracious appetite for literature and I read incessantly. I enjoy Greek classics, Philosophy, Espionage Novels, Vampire thrillers, and several newsletters and magazines.

I try to get a bit of exercise each day to keep my blood flowing. I, on a good day, will walk 10 laps around our track. That equates to roughly 3 miles. I gave up aerobics in February. (Too stressful on my Knees)

I have been successfully tobacco free since November 10th of 2000. This was a major accomplishment for me after numerous failed attempts at quitting.

I'd love to see a photo of you on your bike. I grew up w/a father who took my sister and I on the back of his bike frequently.

I am from Northern Wisconsin, though I've lived all over the U.S. and been in Fla. Since 1991, my family still resides in Wisconsin and Minnesota.

I have a soon to be 9 year old son who resides w/my father. I am divorced as of 98.

Do you have children? Are you or were you married?

I appreciate you do not see my lengthy sentence as an imposition. I too only seek friendships and meaningful correspondence to occupy my time - You'd be surprised at the variety of propositions I've received. !! Then again, perhaps you wouldn't be.

I shall have my copies of my photos in a few days. I shall forward one to you. My hair is a bit shorter than it was last October when the photo for Jail Babes was taken. I'm due to have yet another cut tomorrow. In my book change is not only inevitable, its necessary, even good.

I consider myself a very optimistic, open-minded, non-judgmental woman. I have a kind heart, an excellent sense of humor. I can be very self-deprecating, though I do love myself.

I have an affinity for felines. At any one time in my life I've owned several cats. They are a constant source of pleasure for me.

I enjoy snow skiing, camping, fishing, ice skating, BBQ's, going to the movies, long walks late at night along our beautiful beaches, and going to amusement parks.

Letters from Prison

I was introduced to more cultured activities such as theatre, opera, classical music, wine tastings, and jazz. All of which I'm still enjoying and learning a great deal about.

I have subscriptions to Smithsonian, Bon Appetit, Scientific American Discover, Home Business, and National Geographic.

I fancied myself somewhat of a good cook once upon a time. I can eat salman, seafood, or a good rare steak right about now. I'm far from a health nut, but I do love fruits, veggies, juice, oatmeal, and tuna as a main sourse of nutrition.

I do thank you for your letter and for encouraging me to break up the monotony of my life. It has been a pleasure, and I greatly look forward to hearing from you again.

Take care!

Yours, Paula

Author's Note:

I'd written Paula out of curiosity, as she was in prison for life and certainly not a candidate for employment. The woman came from a wealthy family and had a good education. I made the immediate assumption it was her husband's death that had resulted in her prison term.

May 25, 2001
Daniel,

Greetings to you my new friend. I was so pleased to receive your latest letter and photo. Thank you. Hopefully this letter has found you in high spirits. I myself am faring well.

Your story of how you began writing to persons incarcerated, such as myself, really touched my heart. You are a truly rare person to encompass such compassion for those of us the majority of the populus condemns as the dregs of Society.

I'm one of the few people I've Known !! Who enjoys correspondence w/ pen pals purely for the sake of conversation. I'm not looking for hand outs, nor a husband. The written word has always been a passion of mine and writing letters has become an extension of that.

My story is one I've heard more than once. I was an abused woman involved in a tumultuous Kinship w/a man who seemed to derive pleasure from mental, physical, verbal, sexual, and emotional cruelties. This went on for 2 years. On May 30th 1997 we had a fight that ended in his death. He was shot in the neck. I went to trial on 1st degree murder, but was convicted on 2nd degree. Still sentenced to natural life due to my past convictions.

My dept. of corrections profile can be seen at <u>ww.dc.state.fl.u.s</u>. My hair is white (platinum) and I look like I have a true attitude, but I'm actually quite cordial w/my friends. I've recently acquired a good lawyer who is working on filing my post-conviction, then eventually my clemency.

I will answer any and all questions that you may have concerning sincere approach to dealing w/people the most successful.

It rained throughout most of the day today. Most excellent lounging weather. I slept all afternoon and it was decadent. Very rarely do I indulge in an extended nap. 30 minutes at lunch is usually all I'll allow myself. I've got a pet peeve about seeming idleness. Doing nothing, ie sleeping the day away seems like such a waste.

> *There are always letters to be written, books to be read, shoes to wash etc. When I'm feeling truly lazy, I'll go sun-bathe for a couple of hours w my eyes closed while listening to music.*
>
> *I'm in a new dorm due to some unfortunate circumstances, but I am happy here. My new roommate, Chantay, is very nice. Young, Christian, personable.*
>
> *I would enjoy seeing photos of your bikes; new and old. I do like to see pictures. My contact w/ the outside world was tenuous at best until I began corresponding w/pen-pals last October. Seeing their photos is equally as interesting as those my family (grandma) and friends send.*
>
> *Take care. God Speed!*
>
> *As Always, Paula*

Author's Note:

I was surprised at Paula's bluntness about murdering her husband. From her brief comments, she believed he deserved what he got.

She never wrote me after this letter, although she passed my name on to another inmate. I wish she'd maintained the correspondence. While my curiosity was satisfied, regarding her conviction, the comments about her previous convictions and the move to a new dorm "due to unfortunate circumstances" raised more questions. All I know is, as of this writing, she's still serving a life sentence in prison.

Angela
Dade Correctional Institution
Florida City, FL

July 6, 2001
Hello.

My name is Angela Benson and I received your name and address from my friend, Paula Grieve. She was corresponding with a lot of people and decided to give me the chance to possibly get to know you. She says you are a very sweet man so I'm looking forward to it.

Let me tell you a little about myself. I am 20 yrs old, blond hair, hazel eyes, 5'6", and 156 lbs. I'm in search older, wiser man who has experience in life and is wise, patient, and understanding enough to guide me on my journey in life. I need someone who is willing to share their inner happiness with me.

I'm extremely intelligent for my age as well as very mature. I'm optimistic yet open-minded. I'm active and have a calm and laid-back disposition. I'm a lady and expect to be treated as such.

If you are interested in getting to know me, please, by all means write me back and tell me all about yourself.

Yours, Truly, Angela

Letters from Prison

Author's Note:

Once again, this was an unsolicited letter, my name having been passed on by a cell mate. My curiosity usually got the best of me. I responded to Angela with a modified version of the first letter I sent to everyone else.

August 3, 2001
Dear Daniel,

First, I must say that I really enjoyed your letter and reading about why you write to prisoners. Paula didn't tell me exactly everything but she said you'd be a good pen-pal for me. All I'm looking for is a friend. Someone who is free and can share their life experiences with me as they brighten my day by writing. I've been incarcerated since I was 14 yrs old and in so many ways I guess you could say, I'm trying to be able to experience life through other people's experiences.

Like trips and every day agendas. I want to fill a void as far as life is concerned. That's probably why I enjoy pictures so much.

In the picture, you're on a boat. Is that your boat? What do you do for a living? I'm taking a college credit course for veterinarian assistant, I've taken an architectural drafting course (vocational). And I've received my G.E.D. during my incarceration. I enjoy learning whether it be educational or about general life. I want to be able to always have something to fall back on.

Well, I'm going to end for now with hopes that my letter will catch you at home and not on the road. Hope to hear from you again soon.

Sincerely, Angela

Letters from Prison

Author's Note:

The fact that this young woman had been locked up since she was fourteen saddened me greatly. Knowing she had never, as an adult, experienced the outside world made me realize just how much the pictures I sent meant to her.

I was not, however, so naive as to think she didn't belong in prison. Some background checking showed Angela had enjoyed a short but impressive crime spree, ending in third degree murder, Even John Dillinger would have been proud.

Unfortunately, the last letter I got from Angela is missing. In that letter, she sent me a visiting form. I filled it out and sent it to the proper authorities, but never heard from her again.

Conclusion

As you can see, my attempt to locate candidates for employment at the projected sports bar and grill was educational, but not ultimately successful. Of the women I contacted and with whom I corresponded, there were three I considered possible candidates. My wife was comfortable with only one of those three.

As I'd suspected, many of the women were behind bars as a result of their affiliation with a male counterpart, who was already engaged in criminal activities. While I'm not claiming clemency for any of them – we all have the ability to make choices – it seems the two major contributors to the female prison population were men and drugs, often in combination.

Regardless of the women's past lives and experiences, some of which I learned in background checks and some from their letters, most appeared to go into survival mode, when incarcerated. They used whatever talents and attributes they have to survive. For those in need of funds, a young and attractive face often represented the best solution they saw. In more than one case, the photograph featured on the inmate pen pal web page was a picture of someone other than the person seeking correspondence.

While I'm not discouraging anyone from taking the time and effort to brighten the lives of inmates through correspondence, I am urging caution and common sense, particularly when writing to those of the opposite gender.

Attractive inmates sell photos to those less physically fortunate. Attractive inmates snare a pen pal and then pass him or her on to others, for a price or a cut of the money. In many cases, money is the bottom line. Of the fifteen women with whom I shared more than one letter, nine of them were looking for money and none of them were shy about asking for it. Of those nine, I strongly suspect several were getting money from more than one "pen pal."

While my correspondents were all women, I have no reason to believe it would be much different for male inmates attracting female pen pals, using their bad boy image, combined with remorse and a resolution to reform, to solicit the care and compassion of lonely women, thus attaining funds in a similar fashion.

I am a widely traveled and somewhat street-smart man, generally able to read people I meet relatively quickly and well. In addition, I'm happily married and not lonely or looking for love. In spite of those facts, I found myself being taken in by some of the letters, responding to pleas for financial help, hoping there was more to the correspondence than money. I can only imagine how those letters might have affected me, had I been alone and lonely, looking for love or even a long-term correspondence.

Regardless of my experience, I continue to believe my idea has merit. There are many in prison who have learned their lesson and sincerely hope for a "normal" life when they're released. However, finding potential employees behind bars requires more resources and planning than I'd ever imagined, when I started on the venture.